IGNITE MILLENNIAL LEADERSHIP

6 STEPS TO UNLOCKING NEXT GENERATION LEADERS

Andrew Senduk

Copyright © 2018 Andrew Senduk

All rights reserved.

ISBN: 13: 978-1719285384

ISBN-10: 1719285381

DEDICATION

To my parents: Steve and Selfia Senduk,

I wish you were still here.

"There is freedom waiting for you,
On the breezes of the sky,
And you ask "What if I fall?"
Oh but my darling,
What if you fly?"

~ Erin Hanson (author)

TABLE OF CONTENTS

Acknowledgements 1
Preface 3
Introduction 6
STEP 1 I IS FOR INSPIRATION 15
   Chapter 1 Inspiration At The Core 16
   Chapter 2 Characteristics That Inspire 30
   Chapter 3 Inspirational vs. Motivational 36
   Exercise: Inspiration 49
STEP 2 G IS FOR GROWTH 51
   Chapter 4 Growth Mindset Is Key 52
   Chapter 5 From Fixed To Growth 61
   Exercise: Mindset Check-Up 68
STEP 3 N IS FOR NURTURE 74
   Chapter 6 Nurture The Mind 75
   Chapter 7 Self-Awareness As Foundation 85
   Chapter 8 Build Confidence And Kill Fear 89
   Exercise: Self-awareness 101
STEP 4 I IS FOR INFLUENCE 103
   Chapter 9 Influence, Not Authority 104
   Chapter 10 The Science Of Influence 110

Chapter 11 Thoughts Influence 115
Exercise: Influence 124
STEP 5 T IS FOR TRUST 126
Chapter 12 Trust Is Your Currency 127
Chapter 13 Trust Building Strategies 136
Chapter 14 The Chemistry Of Trust............. 140
Exercise: Trust 145
STEP 6 E IS FOR EXCELLENCE 146
Chapter 15 Cultivating Excellence Daily 147
Chapter 16 Not Above Average 154
Chapter 17 Building G.R.I.T. 159
Exercise: Excellence 163
IGNITE: All Systems Go 165
About the Author 170

Acknowledgements

There are many people who have been of help and assistance, and I am grateful for every ounce of help and support. I would like to give a special shout out to the following people who have sacrificed their time and shared their insights.

I am grateful for great friends and change-makers that were generous to share their insights. I would like to specifically thank Bob Tarigan (@bobtarigan), Jeff Joe, Alvi Radjagukguk (@alviradjagukguk), Gunawan Susanto (@sgunawan99), Reino Barack (@reinobarack), Calvin Kizana (@calvinkizana), Kenny Goh (@kennysgoh), Hanifa Ambadar (@hanzkyy), Rik Lee (@rikleeillustration), Kevin Mintaraga (@kvmin), Victor Chua Kok and Joseph Wadakethalakal (@wadapalooza). You are all my inspiration. Thank you for your time, support and great wisdom.

To all millennials I have had the honour and privilege to work and build companies with, you are an inspiration and there is so much fire and potential in you. I truly hope that this book can be a tool in your leadership journey.

Finally, I would like to acknowledge with gratitude, the support and love of my family; my beautiful wife Melissa, you are my best friend and life partner. I can't thank you enough for your overwhelming love and support throughout this journey. I know I haven't been the most social human being when I was in my "writing mode", thank you for cooping with me. We have spent half our lives together and it feels as if we are just getting started. I love you. My two boys, Rocco and Zion, you are incredible gifts from God. I am so proud of you and thank you for being my inspiration and the reason for what I am doing. You have a unique message to share with the world; go find it. I love you.

Preface

"The distinctive and widely shared attitudes and beliefs of this millennial generation will slowly, but surely, reshape corporations in its image and end the confrontational and bottom-line oriented world that Boomers and Gen-X have created," ~ Morley Winograd (author) and Michael Hais (author).

There is a leader in all of us and we are meant to lead our lives and the people around us. The 21st century represents a constant changing world where the digital revolution has changed our lives in so many ways. Who would have thought that ordering transportation would be 1-click away? Who would have thought that ordering a holiday to a tropical island would be 1-click away? The digital wave has impacted how we live, how we connect and all aspects of our behaviour.

In the background of this all, another phenomenon is gradually taking over the world. It is a movement that is refreshing the workplace, requiring companies to shift company cultures and is redefining leadership in the 21st century.

This wave is called millennials or as some like to call them, Gen Y. There has been extensive research, with a variation of definitions on this age group, but for convenience purposes I will follow the definition that millennials are people born in 1980 - 2000[1].

The reason I wrote this book is that I have seen the impact of the digitalization and "millennialisation" of the world up close and in person. During the last 10 years, I have built companies for millennials and with (fellow) millennials. Some of them didn't turn out as expected and failed miserably, and some turned into multi-million dollar companies reaching global customers and hundreds of employees.

The digitalization and the rise of millennials, call for a different type of leadership, because the digital era shifts views on topics like power, influence, mindset, passion and followership.

I truly believe that leaders don't need fancy MBA titles, millions of dollars in funding, perfect timing, or permission from anyone. Most of the industry leaders and creators of change did not wait for the perfect timing or enough expertise

---

[1] Goldman Sachs Global Investment Research: http://www.goldmansachs.com/our-thinking/pages/millennials/

under their belt; they went for something they believed in. Sara Blakely, the creator of Spanx, built a billion-dollar business selling body-shape clothing but started as a door-to-door fax machine saleswoman. Peter Thiel, Max Levchin and Elon Musk who founded Paypal, the leading online payment giant, were no bankers. Red Bull founder Dietrich Mateschitz started an energy drink business while the soda business was already crowded. But he saw an opportunity and built one of the strongest energy drink brands in the world.

What all these game changers have in common is that they did not have the ideal profile or market conditions to start, but they had a leadership mindset and just executed. They found a problem and lead the way to the solution regardless of their background or circumstances.

Leaders discover what ignites them; they find their passion and fuel their efforts with a sense of mission that goes far beyond a dollar sign. With the right mindset, the ordinary can turn into something extraordinary and we all have that power within, but we just need to find and ignite it.

Introduction

"Hi Peter, how are you mate? Can I have a live price for 50 bucks right hand side cable?" I had two phones in my hands, Peter my foreign exchange trader in one hand and the biggest client in my portfolio in the other. "Cable" was investment-banking lingo for the exchange rate between GBP and USD, and I was about to do a 50 "bucks" million USD trade. My heart was reaching 200 beats per minute, I was sweating and it felt as if there was a disco inside my chest. I was fully focused on my Bloomberg screen that was bleeping and flickering red and green. "1.3475, done!" I was 26 and I just did the biggest deal in my career and could feel the adrenaline in the air.

After finishing my masters in Finance in Amsterdam and a stint at global accounting and consulting firm Deloitte, I landed a job as sales trader at an investment bank in the Netherlands. I bought my first apartment in the centre of Amsterdam, just got married in Bali to the love of my life and life was pretty awesome. I have always believed in the power of visualisation, mindset and dreaming big, but in all honesty, I was not the straight A student. But I did have a vision of how I wanted my life to look like and what type of life I wanted to lead.

After spending the first 5 years of my career in financial markets, I decided that it was time to spread my wings. I know this always sounds so romantic, "breaking free from the corporate chains". Indeed it was liberating, but the fact of the matter was I was going to turn my back to good old corporate life. Goodbye to having a proper logo on your name card (a logo that people recognize and makes them think you are smart without any proper reason), an impressive title (banks love titles), a great salary, year-end bonus, discounts on mortgage and insurance, nice desks and the list goes on. A lot of things were nice. But despite all the goodness, I felt something on the inside that said "Andrew, you need to take a leap of faith, else you'll regret it for the rest of your life".

It was August 2009 and I remember telling my wife I wanted to resign that week. For about 6 months, the feeling of going to the office became less and less exciting. I had trouble waking up in the morning, the adrenaline rush of making big deals was getting less and I felt I was operating on automatic pilot. I even consistently arrived late at the office, while my office was literally a 5-minute bike ride away. Supportive as Melissa always was, she said, "Do what makes you happy, I'll support you." Little side note, funny enough, my wife also resigned the same week from her high paying job as a Creative Director at an international fashion brand. Couples that resign together, stick together right? It sounds pretty insane to me now when I think about it.

So I prepared my resignation letter at a time where the financial markets were a total nightmare. The Dow Jones went to an all-time low, the financial crisis was in full effect and unemployment was hitting the global markets hard. But I always reminded myself that great companies like General Electric, Burger King and Microsoft all started in times of depression and turmoil, so why not give it a chance. I remember my director repeatedly asked me if I was really sure to resign in this time of uncertainty. I was 200% certain and ready to jump. So while everyone was holding on to their job and counting their blessings, I handed in my resignation letter and jumped off the stable corporate ship into the roller coaster called entrepreneurship.

Entrepreneurship

"Entrepreneurship is jumping from a cliff and building a plane on the way down." ~ Richard Branson (business magnate, investor and philanthropist)

I knew from the first day I started working for a big corporation, that I would not be doing that until my retirement. So I started saving 30% from the first paycheck I received and planned for the future. I made a financial plan and over the years I saved enough money to pay our mortgage for 12 months and still have a descent standard of living, assuming (worst case) we were not able to make any income for a year. So there we were, at the kitchen table, we both just resigned and knew things would change big time. We felt a sense of relief, freedom, and excitement mixed with some fear for the unknown. I kept reminding myself; "What was the worst thing that could happen?" If all ventures failed, then we needed to find a job again. Was that really so bad? No it wasn't, so we pushed through.

We went from the famous D.I.N.K. category, Double Income No Kids, to the elite and slightly insane D.N.I.N.K. category, Double No Income No Kids. We went from wining and dining in the most exclusive restaurants and ordering a black metallic Porsche 911 (so lucky I could still cancel that order!), to doing groceries at the local supermarkets and being frugal with the money we had. One of the things I have always learned from my parents was to be grateful for the little things, so you are prepared for the big things and until today, this is still one of my mantras. I have truly experienced that when you change expectation for gratitude, your world changes.

It has been 10 years since I left the corporate world and dedicated my life to building companies and making a dent in the world. In the meantime, I have built a diverse portfolio of businesses ranging from an international fashion brand, a one-man-show e-commerce venture that hit 40.000 USD in sales 24-hours after launch, to raising over 20 million dollars of venture capital and co-founding one of the leading e-commerce companies in Indonesia employing hundreds of people. The red line throughout my career, both in corporate and especially entrepreneurial setting, is that during these years, I have had the privilege of hiring and working with over 1000 millennials.

If there is one thing that I have learned; it is that millennials are the future. They are the buyers, the builders, the innovators, the influencers and the next generation of leaders. Throughout my leadership roles, I have come to the realization that a leader's main responsibility and privilege is to grow new leaders. Simultaneously, the world is changing at an unprecedented pace with topics like globalization, big data, digital transformation, artificial intelligence and social media becoming buzzwords that companies yell around the office daily or even have it painted on their wall as inspiration. Times are changing and so should the concept of leadership. Some millennial facts:

- Millennials, who are already emerging as leaders in technology and other industries will comprise 75% of the global workforce by 2025[2].

- People between the ages 15 to 24 make up almost 20% of the world's population[3].

- Indonesia is currently in a demographic sweet spot, where more than two million people will join the working-age group each year over the next decade[4].

---

[2] The Deloitte millennial survey 2014: Big demands and high expectations

[3] http://www.catalyst.org/knowledge/generations-demographic-trends-population-and-workforce

- Indonesian millennials[5] currently make up more than 50% of the productive age population (those aged 16-64).

- 50% of the Indonesian population is below 30 years, productive and functions as the engine of the national economy.

I have been on a quest to understand more about how to ignite millennial leaders. I imagine a world where Gen Y is not only famous for their quantity but also for their influence, impact and leadership. A world where this growing generation shines and impacts the world in how they lead, create and shape the future. In the process, I will answer questions like:

- What characteristics make leaders in the 21st century inspirational?

- How can you lead without authority?

- What mindset do all millennial leaders have in common?

- What does self-awareness have to do with leadership?

---

[4] https://www.worldfinance.com/infrastructure-investment/with-indonesias-millennials-entering-the-workforce-the-housing-market-must-adapt

[5] Indonesian Central Bureau of Statistics

- How do we consistently ignite and shape next generation leaders?
- How you can grow your trust as a leader?

I have used my own experience scaling businesses and developing leaders, academic research and over 50 interviews with millennial leaders across different industries like venture capital, start-ups, social influencers, creative and design, comedy and the corporate world, to find answers to these questions. I have structured all learning into 6-steps called IGNITE, which is an acronym for:

- Step 1: **I**nspire
- Step 2: **G**rowth
- Step 3: **N**urture
- Step 4: **I**nfluence
- Step 5: **T**rust
- Step 6: **E**xcellence

These 6 steps are at the core of next generation leadership in the 21st century. If they are applied properly, they will plant leadership seeds throughout your organisation and personal life. The two basic qualities needed to see the fruits of this book in your career and personal life, are: 1) a desire to lead and 2) the intelligence to select a tool to help you on your leadership journey.

My sincere hope is that this book will be one of the tools to ignite the leader within you and help you become a high performing leader that has clarity for the future, serves others and lifts the people around you. I truly believe that the most inspirational leaders ignite a spark within their followers that inspires action, so let us ignite that spark!

Your friend,

Andrew Senduk

STEP I
I IS FOR INSPIRATION

"I ALONE CANNOT CHANGE THE WORLD, BUT I CAN CAST A STONE ACROSS THE WATER TO CREATE MANY RIPPLES." ~ MOTHER TERESA (NUN, MISSIONARY)

Chapter 1
Inspiration At The Core

"If your actions inspire others to dream more, learn more, do more and become more, you are a leader." - John Quincy Adams (American statesman and diplomat)

It was a Saturday, just like any other Saturday. We just had our family breakfast and the kids were running around the house but this time, I was glued to my laptop screen. At about 10:30AM I saw in our ERP (enterprise resource planning) system, which shows all our sales and warehouse activities, that the sales broke through the 50.000 USD mark!

I was so pumped that I almost choked in my gluten free pancake and kale juice. Our company was just a few weeks old and for the first time I saw we were moving forward and that the hard work of the team was paying off. This truly was one of the most fulfilling moments I have experienced in any leadership role. Creating something out of nothing and creating unity out of a diverse group of individuals. We were a typical high growth company that had new recruits lined up every week. Any open space, was used to put new desks; it was an exciting time. Looking back, it was an accomplishment in itself to get everyone inspired and aligned by the company's vision. But I knew inspiration was crucial in engaging the team and getting everyone aligned on the future plans. Funny enough, this was a lesson a train conductor taught me years ago.

Inspiration leads to Engagement

About 15 years ago, I was on a train in the Netherlands, from Amsterdam to Arnhem. During this daily business commute, I met the most inspiring train conductor I have ever seen. From a job scope perspective, the train conductor needs to check everyone's train ticket, manage the safety on the train and make sure the train is on time. But this train conductor went far beyond that job scope and was conducting the train as if he owned the train company. He had the opportunity, like we all have, to "wow" his passengers. He had the opportunity to take ownership of his train and leave travellers with something they have never experienced before. This train conductor was so friendly with all passengers. He was singing and checking the train tickets as if we were heading to some tropical destination. By his actions he lifted the spirit in the train and people started to smile.

You could feel his energy spreading throughout the entire cabin, it was a beautiful thing to witness. This train conductor showed me what leadership is about: mindset and ownership. Often times, when talking about leadership, people often think of fancy titles or high salaries. As if your title defines you as a leader. I'm pretty sure that train conductor did not have a "manager" title on his name card. Leadership goes beyond titles and I truly believe that everyone, no matter your title or bank account, has the opportunity and privilege to lead.

You Are A Leader

The word "leader" usually brings to mind a variety of images. For example:

- A political leader, pursuing a passionate, personal cause.
- An explorer, cutting a path through the jungle.

- An executive, developing the company's strategy.

But the fact of the matter is that there is a leader in all of us. Leaders help themselves and others to do the right things. They set direction, build an inspiring vision and map out where the team needs to go. Yet, while leaders set the direction, they must also use management skills to guide their people to the right destination, in a smooth and efficient way.

Leaders Inspire

Being able to inspire is one of the core principles every leader needs to master. To inspire is something different than to motivate. Inspiration translates to "in spirit". Inspiration comes from within. The root word of motivate is "motive," which is an external force that causes us to take action. Motivation pushes you to accomplish a task, or work through a difficult event, even when you would rather be doing something else. We are motivated by a result, an external factor like a year-end bonus or hitting a KPI (key performance indicator). Inspiration pulls you towards something that stirs you from the inside. A person, an event, or a circumstance can inspire.

When we are inspired, we aren't thinking about the final end state. In fact, when we are filled with inspiration, we want to hold onto that feeling for as long as possible.

When we are filled with inspiration, we often don't need external motivation to move forward. The feeling of purpose and meaning is enough to propel us. When we are void of inspiration, we must seek out ways to keep ourselves moving forward towards a clearly defined end state. Those without a clear vision, mission, or purpose often require lots of external motivation to keep moving forward. Those that operate and live from a place of purpose are inspired every day to give 100%. They may get tired, but they can reach back to their higher purpose to be inspired. This is why the most effective leaders are the most inspired leaders and the most inspirational.

Richard Branson identifies the ability to inspire as the single most important leadership skill. The ability to infuse energy, passion, commitment, and connection to an organization's mission and direction is essential in any growing company. According to an IBM[6] survey of 1,700 CEOs

---

[6] Leading through connections: Insights from the Global Chief Executive Officer Study 2012

through 64 countries, one of the top 3 important leadership traits is being able to inspire. In addition Bain Research[7] conducted a study on the productivity of inspired employees versus satisfied employees and concluded that inspired employees are 100% more productive.

It is the trait that creates the highest levels of engagement, it is what separates the best leaders from everyone else, and it is what employees want most in their leaders.

How Great Leaders Inspire

Inspirational leaders have the ability to ignite a spark within their team that drives them to take action. They don't require motivation to act because they have been inspired. So how can you inspire people? What follows is a collection of macro leadership strategies that inspiring leaders do, compiled from interviews, various studies and sources:

1. **Clarity:** A clear future, vision, mission, and purpose. Inspiring leaders know that the most effective way to get people on

---

[7] http://www.bain.com/publications/articles/how-leaders-inspire-cracking-the-code.aspx

board of their dream is to clearly articulate what they believe in, why they exist, and where they are going. They are able to clearly define the vision, mission and values resulting in a purpose. Purpose has the power to improve happiness and productivity, and people need it. One way to do it is to give employees the chance to connect with and meet the people they are serving.

In research cited by Adam Grant[8], three groups of employees in a university fundraising call centre were tasked to call donors to ask for contributions. One of the groups read personal stories from scholarship recipients, about how those scholarships had changed their lives. Turns out that group increased their fundraising by 143% versus the other groups who just made calls as part of their duties. When these same fundraisers were given the opportunity to meet a scholarship recipient and ask them questions for as little as five minutes, their fundraising went up by

---

[8] Give and Take, Adam Grant (2013)

more than 400%. When purpose is crystal clear, it impacts everything.

2. **Collaborate:** Leaders collaborate and work alongside their people to make things happen. One of the reasons why the traditional "command and control" leadership style does not suit the millennial generation is because we value two of the most inspiring words; *we* and *together*.

3. **Integrity And Trust:** Your actions should be in line with your words. Employees take their cues from their leader and to believe in their leaders, leaders must have integrity and build trust. Inspiring leaders know every action matters and lead by example.

4. **Positivity:** Truly inspiring leaders can find the bright side of any issue and see the glass always as half full. They know that focusing on the negative will only make the negative bigger, so they remain beacons of positivity in the face of challenges and failures. Of course, problems happen and troubleshooting is inevitable. But if you want to be truly inspirational, always show others the silver lining.

5. **Listen:** In today's distracted world, this is one of the most challenging strategies. Just slide your phone open and you'll be distracted by pop-ups and notifications. Let's not even get started about social media or email, two of the biggest distraction monsters. Everyone wants to say something, but few really listen. Inspirational leaders truly listen to what is said and respond appropriately, instead of letting it go in through one ear and out through the other. When your voice matters it strengthens a sense of value because everyone participates and everyone is important.

6. **Passionate:** Passion fuels confidence and having enthusiasm for the mission of your organization is critical in being an inspirational leader. Without a sense of passion, work can easily become a meaningless task. Your passion will remind your team about the *why* of their work.

7. **Good Communication Matters**: Without good communication, there is no forward movement and unity. Cutting corners with communication will result in blur messages that cause time-sucking reiterations.

Messages are misunderstood, feelings are hurt and projects turn out wrong. Truly inspiring leaders take time to communicate to ensure that everyone is on board and moving forward.

8. **Raise The Bar:** Nelson Mandela (South African political anti-apartheid leader) once said "It always seems impossible until it's done." This is the true leadership mindset and DNA that inspirational leaders embrace. Setting goals that seem frightening at first but keep the team on their toes. True leaders will lead the way from impossible to possible.

9. **Acknowledgement And Appreciation:** Everyone likes to be acknowledged for their effort. It's in our DNA that acknowledgement and appreciation matter. Inspirational leaders know this and use it to grow commitment and unity. Lack of acknowledgment will result in higher employee turnover, lower output and overall bad vibes. Through acknowledgement and appreciation, leaders can address all 3 fundamental human needs of feeling safe, to belong and to matter. According to Maslow's

Hierarchy of Needs our first human need is to have food and a roof over our head. Once that is secured, every human being wants:

a. To feel safe (a sense of security and absence of fear),

b. To belong (have family, friend or a lover), and

c. To matter (to be recognized and respected)

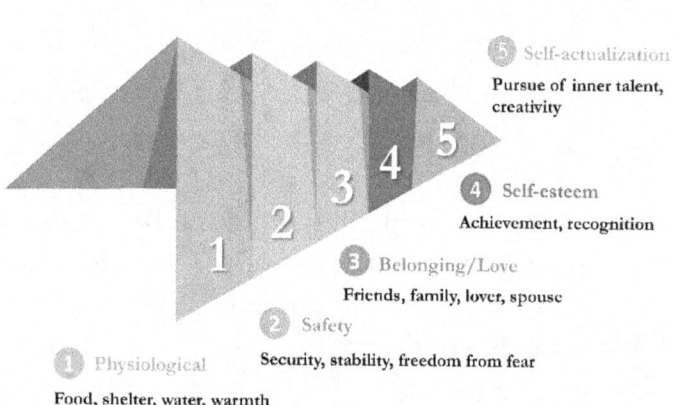

Figure 1: Maslow's Hierarchy of Needs

10. **Care About People:** Being people centric is not just a trending HR topic, but a core principle for inspiring leaders. They want

their people to develop and encourage activities that strengthen physical and intellectual well-being. Developing people is a goal of leadership in and of itself.

The Million-Dollar Question: What Makes Leaders inspiring?

Companies that can answer this question have a powerful tool to increase their competitive edge. Because when we can consistently ignite inspiring leaders within our organisations, we can intentionally impact both the top and bottom line. The power of a company with leaders who inspire at every level up and down the organization is hard to overstate. These are the companies that consistently pull off innovative or heroic feats in business because so many of the employees are inspired and motivated to make them happen. In the US alone, companies already spend 14 billion USD annually on leadership training to reinforce and enhance the soft skills that inspire, motivate and create engagement, but most have found that it is deceptively hard to do these things. Few rigorous methods exist to measure someone's ability to inspire, to systematically develop that intangible quality or to embed those skills throughout an organization.

So what does it take to foster inspiring leaders, not just through a lucky accident of talent management but year in and year out? To help answer that question, we will take a closer look at research conducted by Bain[9], in which they took an analytical approach to demystify the concept of inspiration. The goal of this research was to design an approach to define, measure and develop inspirational skills. Three key questions were at the centre of this research:

- What characteristics matter when it comes to inspiring others?

- How many inspiring behaviours does someone need to demonstrate reliably in order to inspire others, and what pattern of behaviours is most inspirational?

- How to calibrate the strength of those characteristics in an individual?

At first, inspiration might seem an intangible concept but Bain's research identified 33 distinct and tangible attributes that are statistically significant in creating inspiration in others. The

---

[9]http://www.bain.com/publications/articles/how-leaders-inspire-cracking-the-code.aspx

good news is that you don't have to have all of them to be inspirational. You only need four of those attributes, as distinguishing strengths, to be experienced as highly inspiring. Another finding is that there is no one-size-fits-all approach, meaning that inspiring leaders are diverse and any combination of distinguishing strengths work.

Chapter 2
Characteristics That Inspire

"I've learned that people will forget what you said, people will forget what you did, but people will never forget how you made them feel." ~ *Maya Angelou*

Because inspiration is subjective, Bain's research selected a list of attributes to test based on extensive interviews with over 2000 employees and on data gathered from multiple disciplines like psychology, sociology and organizational behaviour. The result was a set of 33 characteristics that are statistically significant in inspiring others. The characteristics were then divided over 4 quadrants that highlight the setting in which they tend to apply:

- **Setting the tone:** Worldview, Openness, Shared ambition, Follow through, Responsibility, Unselfishness, Recognition, Balance

- **Leading the team:** Vision, Focus, Harmony, Direction, Servanthood, Sponsorship, Co-creation, Empowerment

- **Connecting with others:** Vitality, Humility, Empathy, Development, Assertiveness, Commonality, Expressiveness, Listening

- **Developing inner resources:** Stress tolerance, Optimism, Emotional expression, Flexibility, Independence, Self-actualization, Self-regard, Emotional self-awareness

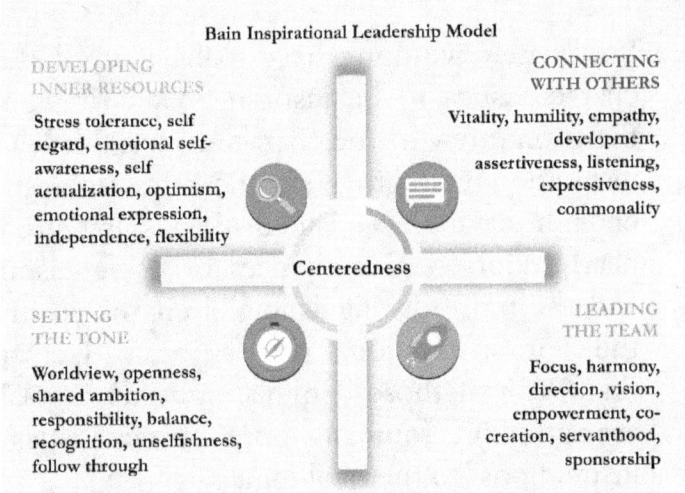

Figure 2: Bain Inspirational Leadership Model[10]

One of the key results is that each of the elements is important to the collective inspirational health of an organization and that no combination is more powerful in contributing to an individual's capacity to inspire. Interesting enough, *centeredness* was mentioned as the most important attribute. Centeredness, which is described as being emotionally stable and secure, is fundamental to the ability to lead and improve one's ability to stay level-headed, handle pressure and connect with others.

The Perfect Mix

Fortunately we don't have to have all of the 33 characteristics to be inspiring. Even if we only focus on a few of the characteristics, our level of inspiration can grow significantly. Interestingly enough, having even one distinguishing strength, nearly doubles your chances of being inspiring, and the more distinguishing strengths you have, the more inspirational you can be. In fact, more than 90% of those demonstrating distinguishing strengths on four or more characteristics are inspirational to their colleagues.

---

[10] https://www.bainleadership.com/leadership-model/

Double Down On Your Strengths

"When people have positive environments, they're more creative. They're more productive. When people are negative, they see fewer options and are less able to solve problems. Negativity shuts down their brain." ~ Jennifer Thompson (associate professor at Chicago School of Professional Psychology)

We only have 24 hours a day and can only focus our efforts on limited things. With that in mind it is more effective to focus on developing your strengths then to neutralise your weakness. On average, investing in adding a distinguishing strength is 150% more powerful at building inspiration than neutralizing a weakness. A growing body of research has shown that encouraging people to bolster their strengths is more effective than striving to fix their weaknesses. According to Gallup's[11] research, the odds of employees being engaged are 73% when an organization's leadership focuses on the

---

[11] http://news.gallup.com/businessjournal/186044/employees-strengths-outperform-don.aspx

strengths of its employees vs. 9% when they do not. That is a big difference!

Building An Inspirational Organization

Traditional leadership programs are only limited to the executives or leadership teams of the organisation. This means that the majority of the organisation is excluded and thus never gets a chance to develop their skills. The key to building an inspiration infused company culture is that leadership needs to reach deeper into an organisation. And the sooner people get started, the stronger and more valuable their skills will be as they rise in the organization.

As technology is infused in today's business and the nature of work grows increasingly inter-departmental, inter-generational and collaborative, inspiration can make the difference between teams that excel and those that lag. Leadership systems that consistently develop inspiration work, because it shows that people are at the core of the organisation. Companies that tap into that powerful combination will have a competitive advantage that few can match.

Without a leader, movements fragment and get nowhere. The leader's job is to inspire people to work together to reach a bigger purpose. To be called a leader, you must inspire your team through your actions and words, and strengthen their commitment and engagement.

Chapter 3
Inspirational vs. Motivational

"If motivation is when you get hold of an idea and carry it through to its conclusion, inspiration is the reverse. An idea gets hold of you and carries you where you are intended to go." ~ Wayne Dyer *(American philosopher, author and motivational speaker)*

Motivation and inspiration are often times put in the same bucket. But there are significant differences and I believe one leadership style is vastly more effective than the other in the long run. For any leader, especially starting entrepreneurs, inspiration plays an important role. Sometimes it's the only thing you have because you can't promise many external motivators like money, a car or bonuses. I remember that when I started my first company, it was crucial to consistently repeat our vision and mission and get the team inspired to make a difference and go the extra mile. It was that same energy and story telling that convinced people to join the company in the first place. Inspirational leaders are intentional in using their position to infuse inspiration and build a legacy. Some key differences between motivational and inspirational leadership:

1. **Inside vs. Outside**: Motivation is typically something that comes from the outside, an external factor like a salary raise, bonus or promotion. Inspiration comes from within, something that has been triggered on the inside and drives you forward.

2. **Long term vs. Short term:** The impact of motivational leadership often times has short term results. Because what happens after that raise or promotion? You fight for you next one right? We keep running after that bonus or salary increase. But at a certain moment the impact of those promotions wear off. Inspirational leadership on the other hand ignites a force from within, impacts for the long term and has deeper roots.

3. **Impact**: Besides the fact that inspirational leadership shows more long term results, it also has a deeper impact on people. Inspiration can engage with people so they feel connected to a bigger cause. External factors can still be an important motivator,

but fundamentally people significantly react better to a heart matter. Good examples are non-profit or religious organisations. The moment people can answer why they follow your mission or why they believe in your company, is the moment you connect with them from a deeper level and it will enable much stronger engagement and commitment.

Are you leaning more towards motivational or inspirational leadership? There is no right or wrong answer, but it's a good time to reflect on how you lead. Are you using a system of external factors or are you inspiring the team to accomplish the bigger mission?

Communication Is Where Leadership Lives

How a leader communicates says a lot how he or she leads. Because communication is connection and inspiration. It sounds so simple but in practice it is one of the most challenging elements of leadership. Communication is critical for building alignment and executing strategy and effective communication is far more than a one-way flow of information. Communication should be a two-way street in which information flows both ways and in every circumstance. When our company went through several mergers and acquisitions, I felt it was crucial to be as honest as possible. Especially in times of change, it is very easy for people to become insecure about the future and before you know it people are gossiping and friction occurs. So it's better to align with the team, even if you don't know all the answers, than to keep everything for yourself too long. Communication is not just about what you say, but equally important is how and when you say it.

Lead By Example

Communicating is about what you say, when you say it and how you say it. But besides the words that come out of your mouth, your body plays a huge role in your communication ability. Verbally and nonverbally, the way in which you communicate has more impact than the words you choose. Leaders inspire others through their words and actions. So before you speak, make sure you listen and observe; knowing your audience is as important as the message you are delivering. Communication should inspire, inform and guide people. Fundamental to effective communication is to be willing to reveal more of you and be authentic. Being vulnerable is key in communication. If you don't show yourself, you will undermine your effectiveness as a leader, and your followers may soon drift to the sidelines.

Vulnerability Key For Communication

When I first became CEO, I was pretty concerned with the content of my message that I failed to appreciate that my tone of voice, my facial expression, and my body language were as much the message as the words I spoke. I was too focused on the form, the protocols and how it all looked from the outside. There was such a drive to be a good CEO that knows everything and acts with confidence. But I've learned that the moment I put down my mask and act more authentic and be vulnerable it made a huge difference. Because the moment I was confident enough to be vulnerable and take off any masks, I became more relaxed in all my communication. From my words, the content and maybe even more important, my body language. People will notice, mark my words.

Why is this important you may ask? Because humans are intuitive and we continuously read and react to non-verbal cues. As a leader, I had to be aware at all times of what I was projecting to others, whether they saw me as confident and optimistic or tentative and worried. Of all the responsibilities of leadership, particularly during challenging times, communication is the most powerful and enduring. Notice the nonverbal cues, and pay attention to people's reactions, facial expressions, gestures, and mood. Otherwise, you could be communicating the wrong message to the wrong people. Always keep in mind that what you don't say may echo even more than what you do say.

Be The Change You Want To See

Leaders are always focused on improving the status quo. They both inspire people and find ways to constructively disrupt established behaviours to help employees break out of culture-weakening routines. The best way to change certain culture is for leaders to exemplify the change they want to see. A few of my favourite, classic examples of iconic leaders that showed the change they wanted to see, include:

- When Howard Schultz returned to Starbucks as CEO, he found out that the company's focus had shifted from customer experience to sales, growth and automation. The first thing he did upon arrival was refocusing the company's efforts back to its' core, the customer. He shut down 7,100 US stores for three hours on February 26th, 2008, to retrain the baristas in the art of making espresso. A bold move, which communicated clearly, what change the leader wanted to see throughout the company.

- In 2006 Alan Mulally came to Ford to help turn around the business. Being vulnerable was an important value for him and in one of the executive meetings he openly applauded Mark Fields (who would eventually become his successor) for admitting to a failure. This set the tone for vulnerability, honesty and open communication as core values of the company culture.

While these are only single actions by leaders, who are famous for producing both performance and inspiration, they provide a window into what inspirational leadership looks like. Eastern philosophy puts it this way:

"If you want to change the way of being, you have to change the way of doing." (anonymous)

Leaders can only change and drive change within the organisation by doing things differently. The more often they behave in a new way, the sooner they become a new type of leader, an inspirational leader. Inspiration is the key to tapping into the full capacity of employees, which is crucial to optimising the most crucial resource of all, human capital.

The Power Of Followership

"He who cannot be a good follower cannot be a good leader." ~ Artistotle (Greek philosopher and scientist)

As a leader, you get to call the shots and you get the credit, at least most of it, when things go well. You are important because, well, you are the boss. Yet few understand that to be a good leader, you first need to be a great follower. Every military general started out as a top private and every iconic athlete started as an eager rookie shadowing the moves of his or her trainer. Being a good follower isn't just about being a leaf on a tree that moves with the wind, it is about choosing whom to follow and transforming the followership into an education.

"Leadership affects an organization's success or failure by only 20%. Followership influences an organization's effectiveness by as much as 80%". ~ Robert Kelley (author of The Power of Followership)

Good followership has power, because great followers are future leaders. So what makes a great follower? Below are 3 mindsets that will transform your followership in leadership:

1. Great Followers Are Future Leaders

How do you see yourself when you look in the mirror? The best followers don't see themselves as another army soldier. They are not "just" executing orders, instead they are aware and intentional of every move they make. They are proactive and are looking for ways to become better and help others improve. They want to know, because leaders are supposed to be on top of the game. The best followers are actually not really followers, but future leaders. That's also how they see themselves and fundamentally has started their own personal leadership journey.

They happen to be self-leaders who follow. Lead from whatever position you are in, do what any good leader would do, lead by example.

Especially in organisations that are sensitive for titles, it's easy to feel intimidated by the lack of positional power or impressed by others position. Be reminded that the personal power you can develop when you hold yourself to a leadership standard is way stronger than any title. The best way to develop into a leadership role is to practice it before you even carry any title. This experience will make the transition smoother and increase your chances of success. When you become a leader, you will have better perspective of the aspirations of your best followers and understand how to develop them.

2. Us Over Me

I'm personally a big fan of soccer. If you look at the best soccer teams in the world and you analyse who usually is picked to be the captain, leader of the team, there is an interesting pattern. The captain is not per definition the person who scores the most goals, but more often someone who can influence the plays and spread trust within the team. Team captains know one truth:

they are only as good as the team. When you make personal sacrifices for the good of the team, you are broadcasting the message you care about us more than me. That sort of selflessness hardly ever goes unnoticed and unappreciated. Team players are the 'glue' that keep the team together. The most respected leaders are the ultimate team players; they use their powerful roles to serve the bigger purpose over their own needs.

3. Believe In Yourself And Your Leadership

It starts with having confidence in yourself and your leadership capabilities, even if you don't have any title or people to lead. You just get things done. As a good follower, you have the confidence to have a dialogue with your leadership. To be a successful leader, you will need to build confidence in your team. Once the confidence is there, you can give the team space to be their best selves, without micromanaging everything they do. You will enable clear communication and are open to feedback on your leadership.

Researchers at the University of Buffalo School of Management[12] have shown that humble bosses are more effective and better liked, so always keep learning and stay humble. There is nothing wrong with being a follower, everyone starts there. But following with leadership intent, is the foundation of growing into the best leader you are meant to be.

Leaders Are Passionate

Every game changer I interviewed for this book has two characteristics in common: passion and purpose. A passion that is bigger than profit and a clear purpose for their life and talents. They are people that want to bring a certain change in the world. People, who really excel in their career or life, have a strong passion for what they do. Passionate people, even though their experience might not meet the requirements, take the biggest risks and make things happen and passion combined with a clear purpose creates magic. Passionate leaders not only care about the work, but also for the people involved. This essentially comes down to an attitude or mind-set, which is driven by progress and curiosity.

---

[12] Modeling How to Grow: An Introductive Examination of Humble Leader Behaviors, Contingencies, and Outcomes, Academy of Management Journal, Bradley Owens (Buffalo School of Management)

Identify Your Leadership Style

When seeking to identify these qualities, it is important to remember that leadership doesn't come in a one-size-fits-all format. Some of the best leaders are full of passion and others are quiet, calm and thoughtful people. But keep finding ways to connect with the world around you, stay curious and have interest in other people. Curiosity and interest are both key qualities of great leaders.

Exercise: Inspiration

Look at the 33 characteristics in the Bain Inspirational Leadership Model. Write down 5 characteristics you think you have and test your assumptions by asking your friends or colleagues:

1. [Example: Recognition] _____

2. _____

3. _____

4. _____

5. _____

Now write down how you can intentionally grow your inspiring characteristics. For example: Characteristic is Recognition. My action this week is to give more recognition and encouragement to my team mates, the mailman or the Starbucks barista and give at least 1 encouragement a day to different people I come across. So write down an action you can take this week to grow and develop your inspiring characteristic.

I will take the below actions to grow my inspiring characteristics:

1. [Example: Give at least 1 person, on a daily basis, some form of recognition]

2. _____

3. _____

4. _____

5. _____

STEP 2
G IS FOR GROWTH

"STRENGTH AND GROWTH COME ONLY THROUGH CONTINOUS EFFORT AND STRUGGLE". ~ NAPOLEON HILL (AUTHOR)

Chapter 4
Growth Mindset Is Key

"It does not matter how slowly you go so long as you do not stop." ~ *Confucius (Chinese teacher and philosopher)*

You might have read or heard it before, "It all starts in the mind". It is so true and realizing this power of the mind is a very important prerequisite to being able to actually create the success, leadership and prosperity you desire. Mindset can be defined as our beliefs or established set of attitudes someone holds. Your belief system gives context to your reactions and tendencies, has the power to define who you are and who you can become.

The Power Of Mindset

Many people do not recognize the power of the mind. It plays a prominent role in everything you do because to accomplish anything, you first must use your mind. If you cannot imagine or visualize something, then how can you possibly achieve it? It is this power of the mind, to focus and visualize what it is you desire, that is perhaps the most important mindset of all. The power to imagine the outcomes you wish for, the obstacles you'll conquer and are willing to work for. This is different than wishful thinking, which literally is about wishing for the best outcome. The moment you strengthen your mindset, you know what you want and hold in your mind a clear mental image of it and see it accomplished. Then you take action accordingly. Strong clear mental images help you to display patience, self-discipline, perseverance and the power to persist in your efforts. Just like a muscle you can train, you have the ability to strengthen and develop a strong mindset.

One of the ways to strengthen your mindset is to plant deep self-talk within the subconscious mind so that it becomes part of you. The correct thought pattern that your mind is not only powerful but is your ultimate tool for success in your chosen area of endeavour. Having this strong clear power mindset allows you to transfer your thoughts to other people who would help you execute your plans for your business or personal ventures. Usually, nothing can be accomplished alone and the ability to bring on board those people around you that are crucial for your success is a must. I remember when I first started our company, I was literally sitting alone in a rented office in Jakarta. Overlooking the hustle and bustle of the big city and scrolling through LinkedIn to find the best of the best. At the same time I was thinking by myself, "Why should people want to join my company?" I did not have any cool beanbags, fancy wall art with inspiring quotes or a buzzing atmosphere in a well-designed open office. None of that! We were renting a very small office, which officially only could fit 4 people, no printer, no cool stuff, just a vision and dream that I needed to sell. But it was this leadership mindset that allowed me to convince and inspire, new recruits to join our company. We eventually did manage to fit 10 people in the small office, talk about efficiency!

People need to believe in what you are doing and saying; be infected with your passion and enthusiasm. Strong mind power allows you to reject any doubts you may experience, take control of your thoughts and strengthen self-discipline. These are mental tools and skills required for success and the ones that ensure success. The power of the mind provides intense motivation and emotional power for achieving success. Increasing your motivation and enthusiasm, enhances your chances of success in changing your life for the better. Your mind power stems from your thoughts, from your words and from your deeds. What thoughts you focus on, tend to come true. Just like the interest on a savings account at the bank that keeps on compounding every month, the effect of producing the same thoughts and images daily, are compounded. Your thoughts become stronger and begin to affect your attitude, expectations, behaviour and actions.

Coincidence Or Not?

No one knows why, but others are able to pick up on thought patterns and subconsciously begin to help you or offer opportunities. Your thoughts seem to create something called coincidence, attracting the right people, places and things into your life. Although not every thought turns into reality, it is often amazing how fate seems to conspire with you for the betterment of your purpose. Use your mind power to overcome the doubts, fears and worries that destroy your innate ability to co-create your world. Ignite your true ability and use the power of your mindset.

Growth Mindset vs. Fixed Mindset

Stanford Professor of Psychology Carol Dweck is known for her work on the mindset psychological trait. She studied the topic of growth mindset amongst today's leaders and concluded that people who believe, they can improve their abilities and skills tend to demonstrate significant improvements in leadership. Like most things in life, your mindset and thinking ability is like a muscle that can be trained and strengthened. Even though you may not be as skilled as others in certain areas, with a growth mindset, you can reach iconic skill levels. The opposite of a growth mindset is a fixed mindset. A fixed mindset assumes that your capabilities are a given fact and there is little room for improvements. "It is just the way I'm built" or "I'm just not a leader type" is something I've heard so often. But the moment people start to believe that things actually *can* get better, their skills *can* develop and that today's capability is not the maximum, is the moment the door to growth can be opened. It also requires people to move away from what is known. A fixed mindset keeps you safe and sound inside your comfort zone. People with a fixed mindset don't dare to try new things and venture outside of their comfort zones.

Yet

Yet, a three-letter word that can give you a totally different perspective of the world. The word "yet" is what separates world-class leaders from the rest. It is fundamental to a growth mindset that believes it can improve skills with effort and that your current status quo is tomorrow's steppingstone to grow further from. It is a mindset that tells you that your current capabilities are purely a measurement of today, but that the future holds more and you can improve and get better.

How To Deal With Setbacks

A friend and fellow entrepreneur Calvin said it beautifully, "Treat failure as your friend". It took several failed ventures before he succeeded. Recently Calvin built one of the fastest growing photo sharing apps in South East Asia by gaining over 30 million downloads without spending any marketing dollars. I have never come across an A-player that has not experienced any form of setback. The interesting part is that all of them went through seasons of setbacks with a learning attitude, which is fundamentally a growth mindset. A key benefit of a growth mindset is that it makes you handle failures and setbacks in a positive way. A way of learning new ways that might not give the desired solution. Everyone goes through downtimes in life, but what separates the iconic performers from the rest is that they see failures or setbacks through a learning lens. People with a fixed mindset tend to look at failures through a failing lens which tears down on their confidence level and their overall performance. Growth mindset performers see failures as part of the process of improvement.

Growth Mindset Characteristics

So do you have a growth mindset? Here are 7 characteristics of a growth mindset:

1. **Embrace discomfort:** You embrace discomfort and are willing to go further than your comfort zone because you know growth is there. Leaders live in a constant state of discomfort.

2. **Welcome feedback:** You are not too proud to accept feedback. Feedback is a tool for improvement for you. Once you

embrace the idea that learning from others and seeking help is a sign of strength, your potential for growth is unlimited.

3. **Get up easily:** When you fall, you get back up easily. Mistakes are a steppingstone to perform better in the future.

4. **Learning lens:** Setbacks are seen through a learning lens instead of a failure lens. You try to learn from setbacks and see how you can improve in the future. Setbacks are a steppingstone to use for next challenges.

5. **Long term over short term:** You choose long term over short term results. Sustainable growth is a long-term game. Leaders with a growth mindset understand the difference and know how to balance long-term solutions and short-term fixes.

6. **Challenge the status quo:** You always want to challenge the status quo and are open to exploring different perspectives and experiment with multiple alternatives.

7. **Listen instead of hearing:** You are a good listener. You are open to hearing other viewpoints and want to celebrate

others for success. You lift others up and encourage them to learn new skills and take on bigger assignments to grow.

Top performers tend to show a growth mindset and it is in reach for everybody. A growth mindset is to look at your business and personal life through learning glasses. Setbacks are part of the learning process and there is a fundamental belief that the best is yet to come.

Chapter 5
From Fixed To Growth

"...I think you can never stop growing, and I definitely take that mindset. You've just got to keep on grinding." ~ D'Brickashaw Ferguson (American football player)

How you interpret challenges, setbacks and criticism is your choice. You can interpret them with a fixed mindset as signs that your talents or abilities are lacking. Or you can interpret them with a growth mindset as signs that you need to ramp up your strategies, effort and expand your abilities. It is all up to you. So as you face challenges, setbacks, and criticism, recognise the fixed mindset voice and let the growth mindset voice take over. When you catch your mind playing tricks on you and fixed mindset thoughts start to occupy your mind, isolate it and overflow them with growth mindset statements. Some examples of growth-mindset and fixed-mindset reactions:

Recognizing Growth vs. Fixed Mindset

Growth mindset

- I'm not sure I can do this, but I'll give it a try anyway.
- Talent alone means nothing. It's the combination with perseverance that creates magic.
- I'll take responsibility for my mistakes. How can I improve in the future?
- If I fail, I'll learn from it and will try better next time.

Fixed mindset

- Are you sure you can do it?
- Maybe you don't have the talent.
- It's not my fault. It was someone else's fault.
- If you fail, you're a failure.

What You Focus On Will Grow

This also applies to the mindset you have. If you feel that your default reaction to setbacks is more leaning towards the fixed-mindset, just be aware of it and start to retrain your mind to respond differently to situations. Remember you have the power to retrain your brain and change your mindset.

Researchers at University College London[13] tried to figure out how long it takes to form a habit. The study examined the habits of 96 people over a 12-week period. Each person chose one new habit for the 12 weeks and reported each day on whether or not they did the behavior and how automatic the behavior felt. Habits varied from "drinking a bottle of water with lunch" to "doing a 15 minutes run before dinner". Interestingly enough the results show, that people need between 18 days to 254 days to form a new habit. This means that depending on the new habit you're trying to form it can take you between two to eight months to build a new behavior in your life. On average it takes 66 days before a new behavior becomes automatic. Of course results depend on the specific new (thinking) behavior, the person and the circumstances. It is very clear though that you can retrain your mind and body through consistency and patience. Just to give some context of the regenerating power of our body:

---

[13] https://onlinelibrary.wiley.com/doi/pdf/10.1002/ejsp.674

- Your outer layer of skin, the epidermis (apart from the thicker dermis beneath), replaces itself every 35 days. Think about when you have a scratch on your arm. It usually fully recovers within 35 days.
- Red blood cells are replaced every 120 days.
- Skin cells are replaced every 39 days.

Over time, which voice you hear becomes pretty much your choice. Next time, when you have a setback or big challenge ahead of you, train yourself to look at it with a growth mindset. This might feel weird at first, but the more you practice, the more it will become part of you and the results will flow. Remember keep training your mind for 66 days in a row and before you know it your growth mindset will come natural.

How Can A Growth Mindset Help You Learn?

A growth mindset will boost your learning curve. In her research[14] Dweck found something

---

[14] https://www.mindsetworks.com/science/

startling: students with a fixed mindset will reject learning if it means not failing. The fixed-mindset group was so afraid of failing that they stopped learning. In this research, one group of students was given challenging problems and were praised for their ability, based on their score. Another group of students were praised for their effort, their hard work.

"The ability praise pushed students right into the fixed mindset, and they showed all the signs of it, too: When we gave them a choice, they rejected a challenging new task that they could learn from. They didn't want to do anything that could expose their flaws and call into question their talent." ~ Carol Dweck (psychology professor at Stanford University and author)

On the other hand, when students were praised for effort, 90% of them wanted the challenging new task that they could learn from. Another outcome of the research was that in the fixed mindset group, imperfections were shameful while the growth mindset group saw it as a learning curve. Same exercise, totally different experience.

Looking at growth versus fixed mindset from a scientific angle, Dweck studied the brain activity of both groups. Those with a fixed mindset were only interested in hearing feedback that reflected directly on their ability, but tuned out information that could help them learn and improve. They even showed no interest in hearing the right answer when they had gotten a question wrong, because they had already filed it away in the failure category. Those with a growth mindset, on the other hand, were keenly attentive to information that could help them expand their existing knowledge and skill, regardless of whether they had gotten the question right or wrong. In other words, their priority was learning, not the binary trap of success and failure.

A New Mindset, A New World

When you enter a mindset, you enter a new world. In one world, effort is a bad thing. It, like failure, means you are not smart or talented. If you were smart, you wouldn't need effort. In the other world, effort is what makes you smart or talented. What is so valuable about the latter world is that it is marked by a passion for learning rather than a hunger for approval. People with a growth mindset have a voracious appetite for learning, constantly seeking out the kind of input that they can metabolise into learning and constructive action. They are not discouraged by failure, but see themselves as learning. Thomas Edison, the American businessman and inventor, "failed" to refine the light bulb so many times it took him over 10,000 attempts to perfect. However rather seeing those attempts as failures, he is famously quoted of saying:

"I have not failed. I've just found 10,000 ways that won't work."

Exercise: Mindset Check-Up[15]

I did this test myself and it was really helpful to check my mindset. I recommend you to take a minute to answer these questions. Remember there are no right or wrong answers here. Just circle the number that fits your mindset. Please answer the below questions:

---

[15] Mindsetworks Inc. (www.trainugly.com/mindset)

PART I
(Circle the button that fits best)

1. YOU CAN ALWAYS CHANGE YOUR TALENT A GOOD AMOUNT, NO MATTER HOW MUCH YOU HAVE.

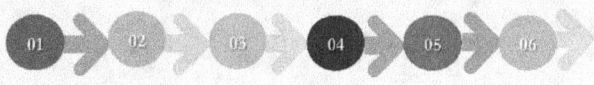

| Disagree big time | Disagree | Kind of disagree | Kind of agree | Agree | Agree big time |

2. I LIKE WORK THE BEST WHEN IT MAKES ME THINK HARD.

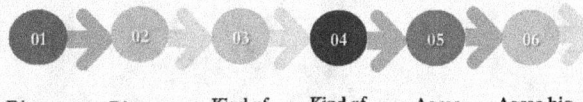

| Disagree big time | Disagree | Kind of disagree | Kind of agree | Agree | Agree big time |

3. I LIKE DOING THINGS THAT I'LL LEARN FROM, EVEN IF I MAKE A LOT OF MISTAKES IN THE PROCESS.

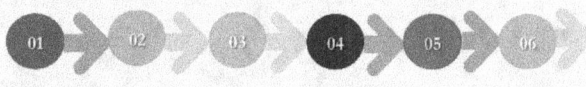

| Disagree big time | Disagree | Kind of disagree | Kind of agree | Agree | Agree big time |

4. WHEN SOMETHING IS HARD, IT MAKES ME WANT TO SPEND MORE TIME ON IT TO IMPROVE.

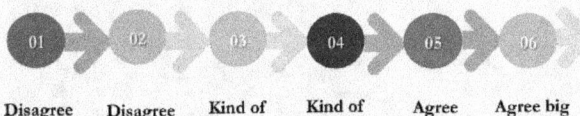

| Disagree big time | Disagree | Kind of disagree | Kind of agree | Agree | Agree big time |

PART II
(Notice the scoring changes)

5. YOU CAN ALWAYS LEARN THINGS, BUT YOU CAN'T REALLY CHANGE HOW SMART YOU ARE.

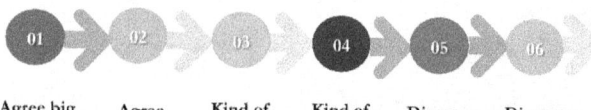

Agree big time | Agree | Kind of agree | Kind of disagree | Disagree | Disagree big time

6. I LIKE WORK THE MOST WHEN I CAN PERFORM WELL WITHOUT PUTTING A LOT OF EFFORT INTO IT.

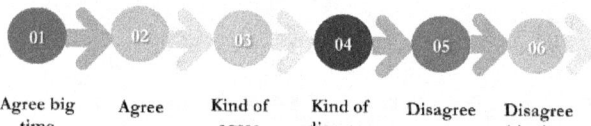

Agree big time | Agree | Kind of agree | Kind of disagree | Disagree | Disagree big time

7. I LIKE DOING WORK THAT I CAN DO PERFECTLY ALMOST ALL OF THE TIME.

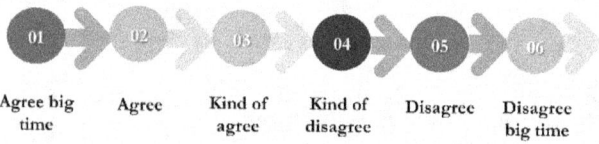

Agree big time | Agree | Kind of agree | Kind of disagree | Disagree | Disagree big time

8. WHEN I HAVE TO PUT EXTRA WORK IN, IT MAKES ME FEEL LIKE I'M NOT AS GOOD AS MY PEERS.

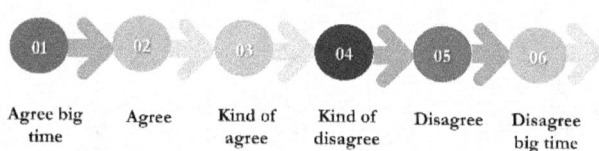

Agree big time | Agree | Kind of agree | Kind of disagree | Disagree | Disagree big time

Mindset Check Up Results

PART I: ....

PART II: ....

TOTAL SCORE: ....

What your score means?:

8-16

You firmly believe that your talents, skills, and abilities are set traits. These things can't be changed very much. If you can't perform really well and look good on a test or project, you would rather just not do it. You think that smart and talented people don't have to work very hard to be good.

17-24

You think that your skills and intelligence probably don't change much. You like situations where you perform well, are less likely to make mistakes, and don't have to put in too much effort. You believe that learning and getting better at things should be relatively easy.

25-32

You are not too sure whether or not you can change your skills and intelligence. Your grades and performances are important to you and so is learning. You are not the biggest fan of putting in too much effort though.

33-40

You believe that you can develop your skills and intelligence. You really care about learning and don't mind having to put in some effort to make it happen. Performing well matters to you but you think that learning is actually more important than always scoring well and looking good.

41-48

You totally believe that you can grow and improve your skills and intelligence. You love challenges and know that the best way to learn is by working really hard. You don't mind making mistakes or looking bad in order to get better.

Please note, that there is no right or wrong score. It's purely an exercise to show you, where you are today. It all starts with being aware of how your mind reacts to circumstances. Once you've noticed your default reaction is leaning towards a fixed mindset, start to take control of those reactions and shift towards a growth mindset. If you're already leaning towards a growth mindset, keep growing it.

STEP 3
N IS FOR NURTURE

"WE'VE GOT THIS GIFT OF LOVE, BUT LOVE IS LIKE A PRECIOUS PLANT. YOU CAN'T JUST ACCEPT IT AND LEAVE IT IN THE CUPBOARD OR JUST THINK IT'S GOING TO GET ON BY ITSELF. YOU'VE GOT TO KEEP WATERING IT. YOU'VE GOT TO REALLY LOOK AFTER IT AND NURTURE IT." ~ JOHN LENNON (SINGER / SONGWRITER)

Chapter 6
Nurture The Mind

"Football is football and talent is talent. But the mindset of your team makes all the difference." ~ Robert Griffin III *(American football player)*

Good thinkers are always in demand and are sought out for their abilities, because anything great begins with a thought, and anything worthwhile comes from a great thinker. Great thinkers are successful leaders. They know how to solve problems, they know how to unleash possibilities, and they know how to achieve the impossible. People who go to the top think differently than others, and they achieve more than most. But the good news is that successful thinking is something you can learn. Here are 9 habits to nurture your mind into leadership orbit:

1. **Plan Strategically:** Simplify the difficult into easy, and translate the intangible into tangible. Planning strategically enables you

to clearly make a path from where you are today, to where you want to be tomorrow.

2. **Zoom-in and zoom-out:** Practice to zoom-in and zoom-out on your current circumstances. Sometimes we get so stuck on our problem because we only zoom-in on our situation which paralyses us to move forward. Practice to also zoom-out and see the bigger picture, so that you're able to take all variables into account. Try to connect the dots and you will always be prepared to grab an opportunity at the right time.

3. **Think outside the comfort zone:** Impact usually starts with thoughts and ideas that go beyond the comfort zone, because that's where the magic happens. Leaders think and dream big and are comfortable being in the "uncomfortable zone". The more you are comfortable being a trailblazer and walk where nobody has walked before, the higher the chances of making an impact.

4. **Be open minded:** Collaborative thinkers like to hear what other people are thinking so they can expand their own ideas. As much as we like to think we know it all,

the best kind of thinking; the kind that brings the greatest return is not done solo but is shared.

5. **Go for the small yes:** Leaders understand how to let people do things they normally wouldn't normally do. A Stanford study[16] researched the so-called "Foot-in-the-door" technique, which basically comes down to persuading people to do something. They went door to door in a small neighbourhood and asked people if they would put a large sign on their front lawn that said "Drive Carefully." Only 20% of the people they asked said that they would put the sign up in their yard. Then, they asked people if they would put a smaller three-inch sign saying "Drive Carefully" in their window. Many more people said yes to this. Then, the researchers came back three weeks later and asked those same people to put the much bigger sign in their yard. This time, 76% of the people said they would put the larger sign on their lawn. These results are

---

[16]https://www.researchgate.net/publication/17217362_Compliance_without_pressure_the_foot-in-the-door_technique

a perfect example of how asking for a small request first will help you get a 'yes' to a bigger request later.

Why does this work? People who first put the small sign up felt they were making a difference. They went into agreement with the researchers to drive safely. In fact, these people most likely felt like very good citizens for putting the sign up. Therefore, when researchers returned and asked for the larger sign, they had very few barriers to break. The homeowners had already been in agreement with the researchers, had already thought of themselves as helpful citizens and they had already changed the look of their house by adding a message. Making it bigger would take very little mental change, and this is why 76% said "Yes" the second time. Leaders always start with small wins to eventually end with big wins. They know that they have to get small buy-ins first.

6. **Embrace the Pygmalion Effect:** If you want to motivate the people around you, put away your cash and open the compliments door. A study[17] by Professor

Norihiro Sadato about social rewards found that receiving praise, not cash, was the best way to motivate participants.

This is counterintuitive, most of our society is structured around using cash motivators to increase our happiness. When you do well at your job, you get a salary increase. When you want to reward an employee, you give them a bonus. However, when researchers asked 48 participants to complete a finger-tapping activity, the groups that received praise for their performance showed a significantly higher rate of improvement relative to other participants. There are two reasons for this; First, the researchers discovered that social rewards like praise are registered in the same part of the brain that light up when the subject is rewarded with actual money. Second, when you assign someone a positive label, like having high intelligence or being a good person, that actually cues him or her up to live up to that label. This is called the Pygmalion Effect. In one study about fundraising, the

---

[17] http://journals.plos.org/plosone/article?id=10.1371/journal.pone.0048174

researchers told average donors that they were in fact among the highest donors. As a result, those donors then did in fact donate above average. Inspiring leaders constantly give their team and those around them genuinely good labels. They want everyone around them to live up to their full potential.

7. **Set huge goals:** Your goals should terrify you just a little bit. According to a study[18] published online in the Journal of Consumer Research, being more ambitious actually makes you happier. Those who set high goals are more satisfied than their counterparts with lower expectations. In the research, one group of participants pick stocks and set a high target rate of return. They were told they could set a rate between 6% and 20%. The low goal setters were not nearly as happy with their winnings and were more disappointed by their losses. Big goal setters were happier with their winnings and less disappointed by their losses. When we set big goals, we get big rewards. Even if we lose, we feel

---

[18] http://newsroom.ucr.edu/2708 (University of California, Riverside)

like we gave it our best try, which is fulfilling in a different way. Leaders never set a goal they know they can achieve.

8. **Decide you will be awesome:** Have you ever wondered what makes someone a world-class singer or iconic multiple bestselling author?

   In 1997, Gary McPherson[19] decided to study musicians, namely, what exactly contributed to a successful musician. Was it practice, genetics or environment? He studied 157 randomly selected kids as they picked and learned a musical instrument. Some went on to be professional musicians and others quit playing after they left school. He was looking for patterns. Were there traits or characteristics that all of the successful musicians had? Amazingly, it was not the obvious ones. It was not IQ, math skills, natural rhythm or even their parents that dictated success. There was only one question that provided a clue to indicate which students would be successful and

---

[19]https://global.oup.com/academic/product/the-child-as-musician-9780198817154?cc=id&lang=en& (Oxford University Press)

which would not. He asked each participant before they even selected their instrument one question: "How long do you think you will play the instrument you choose?" The answer to this question predicted whether or not a student would be successful. If they thought they would play an instrument their whole life, they did better. If they thought they would only play temporarily, they did not play as well.

Their success had nothing to do with skills; it was all about their attitude. We do not need any inherent skills to be able to be good at what we do. We only need an attitude that we are going to stick with it. Our minds and skills will grow with us as we stick to our goals. Leaders should decide and believe they are awesome already.

9. **Be happy:** If you are like me, you have frequently thought, "When I achieve ___, I will be happy." or "After I get ___, then I will be happy." You can fill in the blanks yourself. In my case, I really wanted to have a nice sports car and was researching different car dealers and analysed all features for months. When I eventually

bought the sports car, I was super duper happy for a few weeks. But in all honesty the happiness dripped away slowly. After a few weeks, I started to get annoyed by the high insurance, fuel and maintenance cost. Usually this type of happiness is temporary and will melt like snow before the sun. The truth is, and research[20] backs it; success doesn't bring happiness, but happiness brings success. Leaders understand they need to prioritize happiness because no one else will do it for them.

Act Like A Leader

Something I've heard many times from team members that did not have any "heavy" title, so they said themselves. "I'm not a manager, so I don't know." As if it is impossible to think like a leader if you aren't one. Leaders categorize things and think differently, and you can nurture that leadership mindset independent of your current role. Because you won't know how to deal with things like a leader, until you have acted like a

---

[20] https://psychcentral.com/blog/does-success-lead-to-happiness/

leader. Leaders are vital at all levels of an organization. While the CEO stands as the ultimate leader of the company, leaders at different levels help convey the company's grand vision and motivate teams or departments to meet their goals. No matter what your job scope is, you can start acting like a leader today.

Chapter 7
Self-Awareness As Foundation

"One way to measure self-awareness is by looking at your ability to tell your life story in a coherent way." ~ Anonymous

We live in a society where unfortunately the majority is booing you down for your weaknesses instead of cheering you on for your strengths. After analysing so many game changers, it shows that they are very clear about their strengths and weaknesses. To achieve iconic levels of performance, it is important to know your strengths. If we talk about strong leaders, you might think of a Captain America or Rogue type of person that knows everything and has a clear vision for the future. But after watching Black Panther, it also shows superheroes all have their weaknesses too. Leaders, just like superheroes, are normal human beings with both strengths and weaknesses. What makes them strong is that they are extremely self-aware. Self-awareness is having a clear perception and understanding of your personality, strengths, weaknesses, thoughts, motivation and emotions. Now that we have defined what self-awareness is, the big question is how to develop self-awareness? Here are 4 exercises that will strengthen your self-awareness and spice up your performance and leadership:

1: Kill Your Ego

"It is impossible to learn that which one thinks one already knows," ~Epictetus (Greek stoic philosopher)

I have crossed paths with many high potentials that missed career opportunities because they were too busy proving how great they were instead of thinking about how they can really add value to the company. If you deliver extraordinary results, your talent will be recognised. Don't worry about trying to prove your value any other way. Once you put down your guard (read ego), you can really listen and accept feedback of other people without being offended. This is the start of progress and getting to know the real you.

2: Write Down Your Values, Goals And Priorities

One of the best ways to increase self-awareness is to write down your goals and track your progress. This could be applicable to aspects like your health, wealth, relationships and your spiritual life. Clear goals trigger detailed action, and when you combine this with a timeline, results will flow. It will give you the opportunity to periodically track your progress and see in what fields you need to step up your game.

3: Seek Mentors

Look for people that you look up to, people that inspire you and have achieved the things in life that you aim to achieve as well. Having the right mentors are crucial to your career, personal understanding and growth. They can give you better understanding of yourself because they look at you objectively and know your strengths and weaknesses.

4: Meditate

We live in a time of increasing distraction. A study done by the Nottingham Trent University[21] has shown that the average person checks their device 85 times a day, spending a total of five hours browsing the web and using apps. Therefore it is crucial to find time everyday just to be quiet. I prefer to take 30 minutes in the morning but you can plan it whenever it suits you. Whether it is praying, meditating, watching the sunrise or even doing mundane tasks like washing the dishes, it will help you improve your awareness. Questions you can ask yourself:

- What are my goals for today, this month, quarter or year?
- What progress have I made?
- What do I need to do to improve myself?

---

[21] https://www.ntu.ac.uk/about-us/news/news-articles/2015/11/people-check-their-smartphones-85-times-a-day-and-they-dont-even-know-theyre-doing-it

Chapter 8
Build Confidence And Kill Fear

"All you need in this life is ignorance and confidence, and then success is sure." ~ Mark Twain *(writer and entrepreneur)*

You know the saying about not worrying what you can't control. Well it is something I always say to myself. Although I am a believer in this as well, we humans sometimes still have this feeling of anxiety or fear creeping up in our brain. Let's face it, fear is still a real feeling and these words usually only calm you down for five minutes. But relax, it is totally normal, because it is just how our brain works and the good news is that we can re-train our brain to counteract these feelings.

Fear is Real

Before we discuss how we can manage and kill it, we need to recognise it exists before we can conquer it. In today's transparent world with social media blurring our vision, research[22] shows that the level of anxiety especially amongst millennials has significantly increased. Fear of missing out (FOMO) is a big thing and the reason of a lot of broken dreams. Fear of not being accepted. Fear of not being cool enough. And the list goes on. Since our world is so connected to a level we have never seen before, we need to strengthen and train our brains even more. Because fear is the number one enemy of success and it stops people capitalising on opportunities. Fear has the power to impact your health, literally, can make people sick and closes your mouth when you actually want to speak. Fear, which actually is lack of confidence, explains why we still have economic recessions. Fear explains why millions of people accomplish little and enjoy little. Fear is the *raison d'être* for regret.

Superheroes Feel Fearless

Elon Musk, in my opinion the real Tony Stark and iconic entrepreneur, on fear: "I feel fear quite

---

[22] https://www.forbes.com/sites/amitchowdhry/2016/04/30/study-links-heavy-facebook-and-social-media-usage-to-depression/#f04feef4b535

strongly. But there are times that you believe in things enough that you just go ahead and accept potential failure." He famously was quoted to say that the success rate for Tesla and SpaceX was just 10%. Despite of the survival chances, he still went ahead. "But even if I died or the company would go bust, at least another company can pick up the baton and continue the work." Detaching yourself from the outcome, enables you to step into bravery and pursue your dreams.

One of the late Steve Jobs' primary motivations in achieving success was realizing that one day he would die. In comparison, failure seemed like nothing. In one commencement speech, the tech guru even calls death the single best invention in life. "Remembering that I'll be dead soon is the most important tool I've ever encountered to help me make the big choices in life," Jobs said. "All fear of embarrassment or failure, these things just fall away in the face of death, leaving only what is truly important." Fears and anxiety are part of any road to success; it is all about how you manage these feelings because worrying can affect the body in ways that may surprise you. When worrying becomes excessive, it can lead to feelings of high anxiety and even cause you to be physical illness.

Build Confidence to Fight Fear

Nobody is born with confidence. Sure, there might be some genes that make you more prone to confident thinking, but most of confidence is pure training. So how can we train our brains to fight fear and build confidence? We first need to acknowledge that confidence is cultivated and developed. We often talk about the big marquee leadership qualities like charisma, authority, strategic thinking, and the ability to present eloquently to an audience the size of a filled NBA arena. Good old confidence is as valuable on an everyday basis as any of them. Very few people succeed in business without a degree of confidence. Effective management is no place for timidity. You can get knocked around from many sides. Pressure from clients, employees, investors and other stakeholders. On top of that the ever-present uncertainties of a highly competitive market. It is easy to see why self-confidence is a leader's best friend.

In hard or uncertain times, employees want to be guided by a leader who projects confidence. Confidence sends the right calming message, as do its close first cousins, resilience and optimism.

People don't want to follow leaders who show uncertainty and anxiety. Fear is contagious, as is confidence, but in a more productive direction. As Steve Kerr (NBA basketball coach) says in a quote, "Your team needs to see you as confidant, even if privately you may not completely feel that way."

Game changers, top leaders, A-players develop hardiness in the face of fear. Once there was a man that was a mountain climber, he misjudged his pace and the weather suddenly went from a clear blue sky to a huge thunderstorm in a few minutes. He found himself stuck on a narrow edge of the mountain where he had to stay the night. It was pitch-black, the wind was blowing and he feared of dying every second. As you can imagine, it was the longest night in his life. The next day, when the sun came through, he looked down with clear visibility and started laughing. The entire night he was so afraid of falling 100 metres, while there was a big rock plateau just 5 metres below him. Fear is a mental infection and we can cure a mental infection the same way we cure a body infection, with specific, proven methods. When you run towards fear, fear dissolves. Whether you're trying to become more confident in public speaking, closing deals, leading team meetings or meeting clients, we all need training to grow our confidence. Here are some practical ways to grow your confidence and kill fear:

1. **Practice bravery training**: Put in the hours of practice, practice and practice. If you want to be a great soccer player, you need to train every day. If you want to be a great entrepreneur; you need to try a lot of things (and fail), and put in the hours. 10.000 hours or 10 years is the magic benchmark people need to put in, before the first signs of genius show. So practice becoming fearless. Everything that scares you is bravery training. This could be as simple as starting conversations with total strangers every day.

2. **Release attachment to outcomes:** Oftentimes, we don't do things because we are afraid of the outcome, to more specific the outcome if we don't do it "right". We are so attached to the outcome, that we choose inaction instead. The moment we detach ourselves from the outcome, is the moment we can fully embrace our potential and step into bravery.

3. **Hang with the heroes:** You become your conversations. Listening to an audiobook is like a conversation. Read the books of people that overcome adversity. Be selective with who you hang and choose them wisely.

4. **Embrace the mess:** The things you now find easy were initially hard. All change is hard at first, messy in the middle and beautiful in the end. Welcome the mess. Progress is messy, feel comfortable with it because you understand that it eventually will be beautiful.

Where does Courage come from?

When we have the belief that someone has our back and cares about us, we are able to do extraordinary things. When we foster relationships, we have the courage to do what we need to do. Courage is not so much the absence of fear, it's more about managing fear. Great leaders feel fear but act despite of it.

Born with Confidence genes?

Fear of all kinds and sizes is a form of psychological infection. The first step to kill fear is to acknowledge that confidence; the opposite of fear is acquired and developed. No one is born with confidence. The people that you know that overflow with confidence, have conquered worry and acquired their confidence. And so can you.

Twenty years ago, I did something I will never forget, partly due to the 6-months physiotherapy sessions I had to do afterwards, but let's not get into that. I don't know why but I decided to bungee jump. You know, crazy people that jump of a high bridge or crane with a rubber band wrapped around their legs. When did that ever sound like a solid plan? So I bungee jumped in the lovely party island of Greece, Crete. The bungee jump crane was located at the centre of Star Beach, the number one party spot of the island. It was packed with people and loud house music was banging through the speakers. I still remember vividly that once I was strapped in and the crane went up to around 75 metres, I did not hear any music anymore and the people on the beach became small dots. My fear grew with every meter we went up. The crane stopped and the bungee jump team were counting down, "3-2-1 bungee..." I was so scared and I did not go. It seemed that the fear only grew bigger. Postponement and indecision are like fertilisers for fear. Eventually the bungee jump team counted again, "3-2-..." and before they said 1, they pushed me off the crane into the longest seconds of my life. Suddenly the fear was gone and it eventually was a beautiful, once in a lifetime, experience. Action cures fear. Hope is a start. But hope needs action to win. Two ways to conquer fear:

1. Isolate fear
2. Take action accordingly

Destroy negative thoughts before those thoughts become mental monsters. Any negative thought, if fertilised with repeated recall, can develop into a real mind monster, breaking down confidence and paving the way to serious psychological difficulties.

So how do you boost confidence? Some proven methods that have worked for me personally:

1. **Develop confidence through competence:** The better you become in

for example giving presentations, the more confidence you will build. I remember the first time I did a keynote at one of the biggest technology conferences in South East Asia. There were almost 1000 tech professionals in the venue so I really felt the pressure of bringing good content. I was nervous and a bit shaky on stage. But it's normal, it was my first time. I have come to realise that the more I speak and the more I study the craft of public speaking, the more my confidence grows.

2. **Confidence is both mental and physical:** How do you carry yourself from day to day? Do you stand up straight with your chest wide and shoulders straight, or do you have hunched shoulders and avoid eye contact? The latter body language communicates insecurity and also impacts how you perceive yourself. How you carry yourself makes a difference, not only on how others perceive you but also on how you perceive yourself. It either builds your confidence or breaks it.

   Research[23] from the Ohio State University on the relationship between body posture and the level of confidence clearly shows that posture does matter. "The results show how our body posture can affect not only what others think about us, but also how we think about ourselves", said professor Richard Petty, co-author of the study and professor at Ohio State University. In the research two groups of students were asked to perform similar activities and fill in a survey with the only difference being their posture. Surprisingly students who held an upright, confident posture were much more likely to rate themselves in line with positive traits.

3. **Challenge yourself:** Embrace the uncomfortable zone in all you do. Next time you go to Starbucks, ask the cashier for 10% off. Why? Because it is probably something you are too scared to do, because you feel embarrassed asking. But once we set our default to challenging mode or always seeking the uncomfortable zone, we train our minds that failure is not that big of a deal and that by challenging the status quo, great things can happen.

---

[23] https://news.osu.edu/news/2009/10/05/posture/

Andrew Senduk

You'll be surprised by how much is possible, just by asking.

Exercise: Self-awareness

Japanese inventor, Sakichi Toyoda used an approach he called "The 5 Why's Approach" to discover errors in his company's manufacturing process. A similar approach can be used to get more self-awareness and understanding of what matters to you. A simpler version is called "The 3 Why's Approach". Start with a statement and then ask "why" three times to come to the core of what you find important.

As an example:

Statement: I don't' like my job.

1. Why don't I like my job? Because I feel tired all day.
2. Why do I feel tired at the office all day? Because the air is really bad.
3. Why is the air really bad? Because we never open a window.

You have just discovered you need lots of fresh air to focus. This way, you can go to the core of what you value most not only in your career but also in your personal life. Please fill in the below statements:

Statement 1:..

    1. Why?..
    2. Why?:...
    3. Why?..

Statement 2: :.......................................

    1. Why?..
    2. Why?:...
    3. Why?..

Statement 3: :.......................................

    1. Why?..
    2. Why?:...
    3. Why?..

STEP 4
I IS FOR INFLUENCE

"THE ABILITY TO INFLUENCE PEOPLE WITHOUT IRRITATING THEM IS THE MOST PROFITABLE SKILL YOU CAN LEARN." ~ NAPOLEON HILL (AUTHOR)

Chapter 9
Influence, Not Authority

"The key to successful leadership today is influence, not authority." ~ Ken Blanchard (author and management expert)

Leadership simply means influence. It refers to someone's level of influence; not their level of authority. It is possible to be in a high rank or position but not truly be a leader; it is called being a manager. Leadership is measured by influence; and the level of success that you hold is measured through what you do with your influence. Be driven by adding value to the success of others, not your own.

You Are A Leader

Leading is about the moment of interaction, that split second in time when we come into contact with one another or with our circumstances. In all situations, someone or something is going to lead; the energy, the direction, the intention, the choice, the exchange, and the interaction. Who leads is going to happen intentionally or unintentionally. How are you leading right now? How intentional are you about leading yourself, others, and your circumstances? Think about something in your life that is not where it's supposed to be. Maybe your health, career, wealth or relationships. How are you leading it? What are you going to change? There is no need to wait for magic to happen. You have all it takes to take the lead in every situation.

Leading With Influence Skills

We intentionally built a company with a flat management structure and it's a trend that is happening across industries. More focus on collaborative cultures and cross-functional teams that also influence the position of a leader. The goal of leadership without authority is to get others to willingly cooperate and engage, rather than following directives because you are the boss. In contrast to control-minded leaders of the past, today's most effective leaders are exercising a different kind of power. This new style of leadership is a blend of interpersonal skills that form the basis of a leader's ability to impact, influence, and inspire others. Key interpersonal skills are:

1. Empathetic listening

Development Dimensions International[24] has studied leadership for 46 years. In their latest research with over 15,000 leaders from more than 300 organizations across 20 industries in 18 countries, the study looked at leaders' conversational skills that had the highest impact on overall performance. At the very top of the list was empathy, specifically, the ability to listen and respond empathetically.

"Real communication occurs when we listen with understanding to see the idea and attitude from the other person's point of view, to sense how it feels to them, to achieve their frame of reference in regard to the thing they are talking about." ~ *Carl Rogers (author of On Becoming a Person)*

A further discovery in the DDI report was that only 40% of leaders in their global study were proficient or strong in empathy. And the rate

---

[24] https://www.ddiworld.com/global-offices/united-states/press-room/what-is-the-1-leadership-skill-for-overall-success

may be even lower in the newest generation of leaders. A study by the University of Michigan[25] found that the empathy levels of college students have been declining over the past 30 years, with an especially steep drop in the past ten years. As a leader, developing empathy can gain a genuine professional advantage. So focus on verbal and non verbal communication, and be intentional with eye contact.

2. Warm Body Language

There are two sets of body language cues that people look for in leaders. One set projects warmth and care, and the other signals power and status. The body language of inclusion and warmth includes positive eye contact, genuine smiles, and open postures in which legs are uncrossed, and arms are held away from your body, with palms exposed or resting comfortably on the desk or conference table. One of the main elements of displaying warmth and care is mirroring.

---

[25] http://ns.umich.edu/new/releases/7724-empathy-college-students-don-t-have-as-much-as-they-used-to

Mirroring is nonverbal sign of warmth. You may not realize it, but when you are dealing with people you like or agree with, you will automatically begin to match their stance, arm positions and facial expressions. It is a way of signalling that you are connected and engaged. Facing people directly or rotating your body towards them when they are talking is also crucial. It shows that you are totally focused on them. Even rotating your shoulders a quarter turn away signals a lack of interest and makes the other person feel as if their opinions are being ignored. To give someone your full attention is one of the warmest and most inclusive signals you can send.

3. Positive Vibes Matter

Positive and negative emotions are highly infectious[26], and instantaneously catching them is a universal human phenomenon. In a study at the University of Tubingen in Germany, people were shown photos of happy or sad faces, and a computer then asked questions to gauge their

---

[26] https://www.bus.umich.edu/FacultyResearch/Research/TryingTimes/PositiveEmotions.htm

emotional reactions. Subjects reported corresponding emotions to the photos, even when the pictures lasted only fractions of a second. In business, there is a general belief that people think logically and therefore we try to quantify everything to make better decisions.

But research[27] shows that the centre of conscious thought, the prefrontal cortex, is tightly connected to the emotional-gathering amygdala, which means that no one can make decisions purely based on logic. Logical reasoning is usually no more than a way to justify emotional choices and we're all part of an emotional chain-reaction effect.

You can influence and inspire your team by understanding the emotions that drive performance. Worry, stress, and fear decrease physical and mental energy as well as impair mental agility. Positive emotions; optimism, enthusiasm, and gratitude, increase energy, learning and motivation.

---

[27] https://www.dartmouth.edu/~rswenson/NeuroSci/chapter_9.html

Andrew Senduk

Chapter 10
The Science Of Influence

"One of the best ways to influence people is to make them feel important." ~ Roy T. Bennett (author)

In the late 19th Century, British historian, Lord Acton, famously asserted that "power corrupts." We surely don't have to look too deeply within business, politics and everyday life to find examples that validate this timeless truth. But new research from U.C. Berkeley social scientist, Dacher Keltner, confirms that anyone that is given position of power, is prone to abuse it.

Power Abuse At Work

By 2025, millennials will make up 75% of the global workforce[28] and a majority of workers admit to quitting jobs in order to flee a power-

---

[28] https://www2.deloitte.com/content/dam/Deloitte/global/Documents/About-Deloitte/gx-dttl-2014-millennial-survey-report.pdf

abusing boss. Employee job satisfaction and engagement are at crisis levels.

Machiavelli And Power

A lot of our cultural understanding of power has been influenced by Niccolò Machiavelli's 16th century book, *The Prince*. This book has been one of the iconic books in history to describe the definition of power and up and till today students across the globe still read it every year. It teaches that power in its essence is about force, deception and disregard for people. Nowadays many of us might not relate to the definition of power being about force, deception and disregard for people. But Keltner's Cookie Monster study[29] shows that at times normal human beings, when given power, can be coercive, self-serving or even Machiavellian.

Cookie Monster Study

Three people at a time are brought into a room and told they will be working together to complete a small project. Before the work begins, one of the participants (randomly selected) is told that they have been put in charge. About halfway

---

[29] https://www.thecut.com/2015/01/powerful-people-are-messy-eaters-maybe.html

through the task, a plate of four cookies is brought into the room, and each person is given one to eat. But after the group is asked who should get the last cookie, the "powerful" person not only repeatedly takes it, but also savours it in front of the others. One of the outcomes of the study is that when people are given a little feeling of power, they will become more focused on their own desires than on others. What this experiment confirms is that each and every one of us is vulnerable to abusing power, leading by fear, and stressing people out. So we always need to be aware of this once power or a title is given.

Everyone Start Of With Good Intentions

Research[30] shows that most people gain power by enhancing the lives of others. But when they get into power, there is a pull that leads them to forfeiting the very skills that enabled them to gain power in the first place. They lose empathy, generosity, open-mindedness and caring about others.

---

[30]https://executive.berkeley.edu/thought-leadership/video/power-paradox-21st-century (Berkeley Executive Education)

Dacher Keltner calls this the "power paradox", once people get a little taste of success, they stop doing the things that are foundational to good leadership. All of a sudden, they lose touch with how others feel and treat people rudely. I remember a co-worker that got promoted to team lead and "suddenly" forgot the names of old team-members or started acting all weird because he suddenly had more "power". The ultimate example of the power-paradox.

Focus On The Well-Being Of Others

In todays world power is not so much taken but given. Power is conferred upon us rather than grabbed. We no longer earn power by being self-focused, but by consistently acting in ways that improve the lives of others. Power is nowadays expressed in advocacy, compassion, respect, attentiveness to human feelings, and gratitude toward others. Influence by focusing on the well-being of others can be displayed by showing the following behaviours:

1. **Enthusiasm:** Express interest in others, advocate on their behalf and take joy in their achievements.
2. **Kindness:** Cooperate, share, express appreciation and dignify other people.

3. **Focus:** Establish shared goals, rules, a clear purpose and keep people on task.
4. **Calmness:** Through actions and communication, instil calmness and perspective.
5. **Openness:** Display empathy and a disciplined process of listening attentively.

When individuals use their power to advance the greater good, the evidence is clear that they, and the people they empower prove to be happier, healthier and sustainably more productive.

Chapter 11
Thoughts Influence

"Our minds influence the key activity of the brain, which then influences everything; perception, cognition, thoughts and feelings, personal relationships; they're all a projection of you." ~ Deepak Chopra (author)

Research[31] has shown that just thinking about something causes your brain to release neurotransmitters. These are chemical messengers that communicate with all parts in your body.

They influence your body functions like hormones, digestion and feeling happy or sad. A great example is the Placebo effect, as can be seen with fake operations or drugs. They work because of the power of thought. Expectancies and associations have been shown to change the brain chemistry, which transforms into actual

---

[31] The Intention Experiment: Using Your Thoughts to Change Your Life and the World, Lynne McTaggart

physiological and cognitive outcomes such as less anxiety, increased immune system and elevated hormone levels.

A thought is not only a thing; a thought is a thing that influences other things. ~ Lynne McTaggart (author)

Your Thoughts Sculpt Your Brain

Every thought that crosses your mind causes neurochemical changes. Negative thoughts can cause feelings of anxiety and stress. Positive thoughts can give you a sense of peace or inspiration. Every morning, before I start the day, I always take 3 minutes to be grateful. I think about 3 things I am grateful for and think about it and just meditate on it. This could be that I am alive, I have a roof over my head and that I had an inspiring discussion with a good friend yesterday. It can be anything. By consciously practicing gratitude, you get a bunch of rewarding neurotransmitters, like dopamine, shot through your body. As a result, you will experience a general alerting and brightening of the mind.

What flows through your mind also sculpts your brain in permanent ways. The mind is like the movement of information that runs through your nervous system, which on a physical level is the electrical signal running back and forth. As a thought travels through your brain, neurons fire together in distinctive ways based on the specific information being handled, and those patterns of neural activity actually change your neural structure.

A thought is an electrochemical event, taking place in your nerve cells producing a cascade of physiological changes. If you have been overflowing your cells with negative thoughts, you are literally programming your cells to receive more of the same negative peptides in the future. This way, you are lessening the number of receptors of positive peptides on the cells, making yourself more inclined towards negativity. Every cell in your body is replaced about every two months and we have the power to reprogram our cells and thus our body. Reprogram your cells to be more optimistic by adopting positive thinking practices, like mindfulness and gratitude.

Speak To Your Genes

Every thought that crosses your mind is speaking to your genes. It is a generally accepted thought that you are the product of your past. The seeds for how we react to certain things like disappointments, stressful situations or conflicts might have been planted in our past. But this does not mean we don't have the power to change this. About 5% of gene mutations are thought to be the direct cause of health issues[32]. That leaves 95% of genes linked to disorders as acting as influencers, which can be influenced one way or another. These could be childhood events, diet, stress and emotional states.

Your biology does not determine your destiny. Genetic activity is largely determined by your thoughts, attitudes and perceptions. Epigenetics, the study of changes in organisms caused by modification of gene expression rather than alteration of the genetic code itself, is proving that your perceptions and thoughts control your biology, which places you in the driver's seat. By changing your thoughts, you can influence and shape your own genetics. You always have a choice in determining what input your genes receive because input is output.

You have the power to influence your physical and mental realities. Never underestimate the

---

[32] http://genetics.thetech.org/about-genetics/mutations-and-disease

power of your mindset and thoughts. Your body, to the gene level, recognizes it. The stronger your mental habits are, the stronger your body will become. We don't have the power to change our past, but we have the power and ability to shape our brains and genes, and by doing so shape our future.

Cleaning Hotel Rooms vs. Cleaning Hotel Rooms

Human beings have the tendency to think that our bodies respond to physical exercise in a mechanical way. We count our calorie intake and the calories we lose on a treadmill. Who is with me? However, merely changing our thoughts about our physical activity seems capable of changing our bodies. In a Harvard Study[33] on the physical impact of cleaning hotel rooms, 2 groups of hotel cleaners were monitored. Hotel room attendants clean on average 15 rooms per day, each room taking between 20 and 30 minutes to complete. The physical activity involved meets the general recommendation of at least 30

---

[33] https://dash.harvard.edu/bitstream/handle/1/3196007/langer_excersiseplaceboeffect.pdf?sequence=1

minutes of physical exercise per day for a healthy lifestyle.

Group 1 was informed that their work provided the recommended exercise for a healthy lifestyle. Group 2 did not get this information and was doing their shifts like normal. The groups were monitored for 4 weeks. People in group 1 lost weight; their body fat percentages went down, waist-to-hip ratios improved, and blood pressures dropped. People in group 2 showed no such improvement. These changes occurred despite the fact that the hotel room attendants' amount of work, amount of exercise outside of work, and diets stayed the same. How you think not only impacts your inside, but also your outside.

How to Increase Your Influence

1. Emotionally Connect With People

The key to influence is dopamine. If you want to intrigue and influence people, you have to get their dopamine pumping. Dopamine stimulates that pleasure-reward area in the brain that makes people feel all warm and fuzzy. Influencing people is about stimulating this part of the brain. A great way to do that is by having excellent conversation starters handy. Asking interesting questions is a good way to truly connect with people. You can ask them:

What was the best part of your day and why?

What personal passion project are you currently working on right now?

2. Be Emotionally Curious

When you make others feel important, your influence goes a long way. Everyone wants to be liked, loved and accepted. When you fulfil that need for others, you are perceived as being influential. Become genuinely interested in other people. A great way to do this is to ask them open-ended questions. Get people talking about themselves and that will help you build rapport.

3. Let The Body Talk

Influence with your body language. Low-powered body language is normally contracted, with the shoulders rolled and the head down or bowed. High-powered or confident body language is expansive. The head is held high, the arms are loose, the shoulders are set back and the chest is out. When you manifest powerful body language, you are seen as more influential. Confident body language not only affects the way others see you but also the way you see yourself.

4. Tell A Story

People love stories. We are almost hard-wired for stories. When people hear stories, they can feel as if they are right there with the other person. It is like the listener is experiencing the story along with the narrator. Do you see the potential of how influential storytelling could make you? When someone tells a story, the brain of the listener will be in sync with the storyteller. If you can stimulate the other person's brain with a story, you can, in effect, get that person on your side.

5. Be Vulnerable

Being open about your emotions increases your likeability and influence. People will perceive you as being real when you admit to weaknesses or flaws. Some people are fearful because of something called the spotlight effect, thinking that others are paying more attention to them than they truly are. But the opposite is true. People are able to better relate to you when you open up. Sharing a vulnerable story from your story toolbox enables you to connect better with other people. By doing this, you not only tell a great story but you also are being vulnerable, so it increases your influence in two ways.

6. Become Charismatic

Who is the most charismatic person you know? Why did you pick that person? Most likely you chose that individual because of the way that person makes you feel. People often times don't remember what an individual looks like or what he or she might have said. But they always remember how the individual made them feel. Charismatic people make others feel good. Easy ways to score points on your charisma when talking to someone is to: tilt your head, align your torso with that person's body posture and point your toes toward the person. This will bring you in the right "charisma zone".

Exercise: Influence

Body language is crucial in connecting and influencing people. Communicating is both verbal and non verbal. If we are more aware of how our body language also communicates, you'll be a better communicator. Some things you can try next time you talk with someone:

1. Always keep eye contact when talking to people.
2. Talk to at least 1 random stranger per day and ask an open question, like:
    a. What was the most recent funny movie you saw? And what did you like about it?
    b. How would you describe yourself in 3 words?
3. Mirror how they stand and talk (don't make this too evident, else they will think you are crazy).

Action

[Example: Keep making eye-contact]

1:..
2:..
3:..

Results

[Example: Deeper connection with people]

1:..
2:..
3:..

STEP 5
T IS FOR TRUST

"TRUST IS THE GLUE OF LIFE. IT'S THE MOST ESSENTIAL INGREDIENT IN EFFECTIVE COMMUNICATION. IT'S THE FOUNDATIONAL PRINCIPLE THAT HOLDS ALL RELATIONSHIPS." ~ STEPHEN R. COVEY (EDUCATOR, AUTHOR AND MANAGEMENT EXPERT)

Chapter 12
Trust Is Your Currency

"Trust is like blood pressure. It's silent, vital to good health, and if abused it can be deadly." ~ Frank Sonnenberg (author)

When you are intentional with certain trust behaviours, you will be able to make deposits into the "trust account" of another party. To become a trust dealer, you can develop your trust fundamentals:

- **Self-Trust:** The confidence you have in yourself. Trust in your ability to set and achieve goals, to walk your talk, and also be aware you have the ability to inspire trust in others.

- **Relationship Trust:** How to establish and increase the trust accounts we have with others. The job of a leader is to go first, to extend trust first. Not a blind trust without expectations and accountability, but rather a "smart trust" with clear expectations and strong accountability built into the process. The best leaders always lead with an intention to trust, as opposed to an intention not to trust.

Trust cannot become a performance multiplier unless the leader is prepared to go first." ~ Craig Weatherup (former CEO PepsiCo)

The best leaders recognize that trust impacts 24/7, 365 days a year. It undergirds and affects the quality of every relationship, every communication, every work project, every business venture, and every effort in which we are engaged. It changes the quality of every present moment and alters the trajectory and outcome of every future moment of our lives, both personally and professionally. In every situation, nothing is as fast, as the speed of trust.

The Impact of Low Trust

The world needs more trust. Just looking at the headlines in the newspapers, it is clear to me that the world needs more trust. Trust in our world leaders, financial markets, job market and our economy. Research[34] shows that only 49% of employees trust senior management, and only 28% believe CEOs are a credible source of information. Indeed, "trust makes the world go round," and right now, we are experiencing a crisis of trust. Especially in the 21st century, where there is an information overload, trust is something we need to handle with care. This trust crisis triggers three important questions:

- What are the financial consequences of low trust?
- Can you measure the upside of trust?
- How can the best leaders build trust within their organizations to reap the benefits?

Most people don't know how to think about the organizational and societal consequences of low trust because they don't know how to quantify or measure the cost. For many, trust is intangible, subjective and unquantifiable. If it remains that way, then people don't know how to get their arms around it or how to improve it. But the fact is; the costs of low trust are very real, they are quantifiable, and they are staggering.

Trust Tax and Dividend

---

[34] The business case for trust, Stephen Covey (Chief Executive Magazine, June 2007)

Lack of trust has the power to destroy or limit potential of any undertaking. The best way to understand the impact of low trust is to recall that specific relationship you had where there was a lack of trust. Maybe an old boss, colleague or personal relationship you had in the past. How did that make you feel? Were you able to fully engage in that relationship or were you holding back? When trust is low it places a hidden "tax" on every communication and every interaction. Every decision is taxed, bringing speed down and sending costs up. My experience is that significant distrust triples the time for things to get done and thus pushes cost up. By contrast, individuals and organizations that have earned and operate with high trust, experience the opposite of a tax, a dividend that is like a performance multiplier, enabling them to succeed in their communications and move with incredible speed.

A recent Watson Wyatt study[35] showed that high trust companies outperform low trust companies by nearly 300%. The ability to establish, grow, and restore trust among stakeholders is a critical competency of leadership needed in the 21st

---

[35] https://chiefexecutive.net/the-business-case-for-trust/

century. Building trust is, in fact, a competency that can be learned, applied, and understood. It is something that you can get good at, something you can measure and improve, and something that can "move the needle." Leaders are hope and trust dealers and need it to be fully effective.

"Leadership without mutual trust is a contradiction in terms." ~ Warren Bennis (author and leadership expert)

Character and Competence

So how do the best leaders build trust? One of the core focus points of any leader is to build and inspire trust. Trust is confidence born of two dimensions: character and competence. Character includes your integrity, motive, and intent with people. Competence includes your capabilities, skills, results, and track record. Both dimensions are vital. With increasing transparency and focus on ethics in our digital society, the character side of trust is fast becoming the price of entry in the new global economy. However, the differentiating and often ignored side of trust, competence, is equally essential. You might think a person is sincere, even honest, but you won't trust that person fully if he or she doesn't get results. And the opposite is also true.

A person might have great skills and talents and a good track record, but if he or she is not honest, you are not going to trust that person either. The best leaders begin by framing trust in economic terms for their companies. When an organization recognizes that it has low trust, huge economic consequences can be expected. Everything will take longer and cost more because of the steps organizations will need to take to compensate for their lack of trust. Suddenly leaders recognize how low trust is not merely a social issue, but that it is an economic matter and impacts the bottom line of the company. The dividends of high trust can be similarly quantified, enabling leaders to make a compelling business case for trust. The best leaders then focus on making the creation of trust an explicit objective and a goal that is focused on, measured, and improved. It must be communicated that trust matters to management and leadership. One of the best ways to do this is to make an initial baseline measurement of organizational trust and then to track improvements over time. True trust transformation starts with building credibility at the personal level.

The Foundation of Trust

Where trust is an objective fact, it comes down to if what you say is what you do. Credibility is more subjective; because it depends on the way you present yourself and other people's perception of you. Your level of trust is built on your own credibility, and it can be a real differentiator for any leader. A person's reputation is a direct reflection of their credibility, and it precedes them in any interaction or negotiation they might have. When a leader's credibility and reputation are high, it enables them to establish trust fast and as a result speed goes up, and cost goes down. Credibility is built on 4 pillars:

- Integrity
- Intent
- Capabilities
- Results

Integrity

Do you only talk the talk, or do you also walk the talk? Credibility goes hand in hand with integrity. Integrity is about honesty and being consistent, inside and out. It is about acting the same behind closed doors as you would on a platform. The way you act should be in line with your values and beliefs. You are not afraid to speak up or say "no" if it is not in line with your values.

Intent

What are your intentions? This is about your motives and the why behind your actions. Trust is the positive outcome of straightforward actions based on mutual benefit. The moment we doubt someone's agenda or we don't believe their intentions, credibility is lost.

Capabilities

If I would pass a soccer ball to Christiano Ronaldo (arguably the best soccer player in the world), I am confident he would score an amazing goal. The same applies when I would pass a basketball to Lebron James (arguably the best basketball player in the world), there would be no doubt in my mind he would score. Capabilities matter and support your credibility. We all have abilities to inspire confidence: our talents, attitudes, skills, knowledge and style. They are the tools we use to produce results. A great CEO that has integrity and whose intentions are good, but can't lead a company will not have a long career. Capabilities impact our ability to establish, grow and restore trust.

Results

Results build trust. What is your track record or what track record are you building? When we accomplish what we are expected to do, it builds our credibility. Think about your team member that you know you can trust and always delivers what he or she promises to do. Results matter and are key trust components.

Chapter 13
Trust Building Strategies

"The best way to find out if you can trust somebody is to trust them." ~ Ernest Hemingway (novelist and journal)

Whether you are building a start-up, leading a team in a corporation, or working in a non-profit, building trust is a core element of success. The moment you start building a team, it is about achieving goals together and working efficiently. Trust allows you to delegate certain tasks without being worried if it will be done or not. Trust enables open communication and foremost triggers leadership and accountability. Below are 4 ways to build trust in your organisation:

1. Chill

Sounds easy right? The moment you delegate and really trust a person to take action, don't be too uptight. As a young consultant I had one intern under my wings. I was more hyped about having someone "under" me than actually trying to help grow the intern. I was very focused on delegating and micro managed everything he did. I was more focused on the outcome than actually giving him space to show what he could do. Stay calm and flexible about the result. If you let someone follow up on a task, he or she will do it different from how you would do it. So the outcome could be different. If that is the case, relax and discuss what can be done differently. But in all situations, just chill and don't be too uptight with the outcome, but be more focused on building trust with your team and the learning that can be shared afterwards.

2. Be Real

One of the best ways to build trust is for leaders to show who they really are. Be real, be you. Sometimes there is a sense that leaders cannot be vulnerable because they need to be the captain of the ship. If you make yourself vulnerable and express something in confidence to your team, they will be more inclined to do the same. Lead by example because leaders should serve as role models. The more transparent you are in your actions, the more transparent your team will be in theirs.

3. Speak Up

Trust and openness go hand in hand. The best company culture is the one where people are not afraid to speak up and get into the conversation. Team members should be encouraged to share their thoughts and opinions. For example, during meetings, ask everyone to share their thoughts. Leaders should facilitate a conversation by allowing everyone to share their opinions. This way, you build a culture where everyone shows interest, participates and listens to each other.

4. Build Relationships

Building trust in any relationship takes time. Do you trust your best friend? Do you trust your teammates from the sports team? The same applies to your colleagues at work. Why would you not build proper relationships with the people you spend 40 hours a week with? Periodically invest in less formal activities which are not work related so that the team can really get to know each other outside of the office context. Team members need to get to know each other on a personal level. Does it mean, they all need to be BFF's (best friend forever)?

No. But if they trust and support one another and better understand each other's strengths and weaknesses, your company is set for success.

Chapter 14
The Chemistry Of Trust

"Whoever is careless with the truth in small matters cannot be trusted with important matters." ~ Albert Einstein *(physicist, smartest dude ever)*

Oxytocin is a neuropeptide, which is a small protein-like molecule (peptide) used by neurons to communicate with each other, that increases our ability to trust. Oxytocin acts as the neuro-mechanism for groups, clubs and tribes. It bonds people together and, at the same time, creates boundaries between those we are bonded to and those we are set against. What do hooligans, investment bankers, start-up entrepreneurs and street gangs have in common? At first you would say these groups have nothing in common, but looking at them from a social behaviour angle, there is one thing that they have in common: trust.

All of these groups have been through a lot together, whether it be working on a big project, building a company from the ground up or preparing for a big fight (literally). Have you ever done over-time together with colleagues to finish a project and in the process got to know them better? At the end of it, you don't just feel accomplished for pulling off that project, you feel a sense of affiliation with them; you trust them more. Sometimes, just surviving the ordeal together creates this type of bond. When this bond or affiliation is created, oxytocin is released in the brain and unlocks each individual's ability to trust one another.

Touch Releases Oxytocin

Your brain has a huge "trust safe" that can only be opened by oxytocin keys. When you touch someone's hand, it sends oxytocin racing through both your brains, unlocking your trust safe. Hundreds of thousands of locks spring open in milliseconds and this giant safe swings open. Behind that door is your ability to trust another person or feel intense jealousy towards them, depending on the context.

Creating Affiliation Builds Trust

Fortunately, there is another way to tap into the way our brains decide whom and how to trust others in order to resolve conflicts. There is power in what psychologists call "affiliation", which refers to the emotional connection an individual feels with another person. Stable constructive connections tend to produce positive emotions and a desire to cooperate. Affiliation with someone releases oxytocin, much the same way that touch does. So the more we create affiliation, relevance or a shared passion, the more we unlock our ability to be trusted. In any conflict between deeply divided groups, creating a sense of affiliation between them will trigger oxytocin to be released in their brains and unlock each individual's ability to start to trust one another.

The Brain Based Way To Trust

As a leader dealing with conflict, you don't have to touch and hug everyone, but you do have to create a sense of affiliation. Here is how:

1. Appreciate their value

Let someone know that you see what he or she brings to the team. It is important to note you can't make this up. You have to know that they make people laugh, drive projects toward deadlines on time or discover novel ways around obstacles. When you appreciate the value someone genuinely brings to your team, they feel seen. And when they feel seen, they feel connected to you. It starts with empathy and evolves into relationship and engagement.

2. Share a story

Share something about yourself that does not have to do with the conflict at hand, maybe an anecdote from your childhood, your wedding, or something that happened with your kids. You don't have to be deeply vulnerable but simply sharing something very human creates a sense of our common humanity and increases a sense of affiliation. The emotional tone of the conversation will shift.

3. Get into their narrative

Understand where they are coming from. Set aside how you feel and the points you want to make. Set aside what you believe is right and wrong. Only try and understand the other person's point of view: Where are they coming from? What are the stories they remember that might inform their point of view? It starts with empathy, but it doesn't end there. You have to engage the other person and ask them questions like: What happened? What did you see? What did you hear? What do you know to be true? You do not argue, do not interrupt and just listen. In listening, you will come to understand where the other person's beliefs, expectations, and frustrations arise. The oxytocin keys in your brain will release. In being listened to, the other person's oxytocin keys will release. In the end, you will both be more open to trusting each other than you were initially.

Exercise: Trust

The next time you commit to something, really do it! This is the best way you will start to grow your credibility, and people will trust you more. Write down 3 things you will commit to this week, personally or in business. Example: Respond to emails within 24 hours. Action: Give feedback within 24 hours on all emails. If you don't have an answer yet, let the sender know you are working on it and give a timeline for proper feedback. In the coming week, I will commit to:

1. _____

2. _____

3. _____

Andrew Senduk

STEP 6
E IS FOR EXCELLENCE

"PERFECTION IS NOT ATTAINABLE, BUT IF WE CHASE PERFECTION, WE CAN CATCH EXCELLENCE." ~ VINCE LOMBARDI (AMERICAN FOOTBALL PLAYER AND COACH)

Chapter 15
Cultivating Excellence Daily

"We are what we repeatedly do. Excellence then, is not an act but a habit." ~ Aristotle (Greek philosopher)

Habits form the foundations for how we live, work and play. Whether or not, we are intentional about them, our habits shape who we become. Where are your habits leading you? We all have habits and daily routines; many we aren't even aware of. However, due to the power of habits in our lives, we would be wise if we choose our habits intentionally.

Habits, Habits, Habits

Five years ago, my habits were clearly not setting me up for long-term success. Thankfully, I have been more intentional and have been cultivating habits that will pay off for years to come. Your daily habits shape the trajectory of your life. Consider how many of them you may already be doing or which ones you would like to put into action more consistently. These are just some habits, which have been a huge game changer for me personally:

1. Be An Early Riser

This is one of the toughest habits I have developed and in all honesty I still sometimes struggle with. Yet, it does pays off every single time. Starting my day at 6:00 AM provides me with some guaranteed quiet time before the kids come jumping on my bed. It also makes me feel like I get a head start on the day, pursuing excellence before other people even wake up. The other side of the medal is that you should go to bed early as well. It doesn't make sense to me to go to bed at 1:00AM and then wake up 5 hours later. I tried this "hustle guru" method, but it did not work for me. So just try things for yourself and see what works. I usually try to hit the bed around 23:00.

2. Start Every Day with a Power-Packed Morning Ritual

My morning ritual is one of my favourite parts of the day. This is really when I invest in myself, feeding my mind and body. My morning ritual is

1 hour long. Regardless the time you have, use it to start your day with high impact activities like prayer, reading, journaling, exercise, meditation or eating breakfast. The point is to be intentional with how you start your day.

3. Live With Purpose

We were made for a life of excellence. When we pursue that excellence daily, we live with passion and we operate from our sweet spots. My purpose and passions have become clearer to me over the last few years. It takes intention and effort to get clarity on these matters, but it is so worth it. Now, I look forward to welcoming each morning and feel more continuity and fulfilment in my life.

4. Exercise

If we want to be our best selves, we have to cultivate a habit of exercise. Exercise strengthens us physically and mentally. People who exercise regularly feel better, are healthier, cope better with stress and adversity and are more successful than those who don't. Research[36] found exercise

---

[36] https://www.ncbi.nlm.nih.gov/pmc/articles/PMC3674785/

to be just as good, if not better, than medications for forms of anxiety and depression. All it takes is a minimum of 3 – 4 days of 30 minutes of sweat producing activity and you'll clear your mind and have a better view on how your future will look like.

5. Sleep Well

In this age where everybody wants to "hustle", sleep is sometimes a underrated. If you are not regularly getting enough sleep, you are probably experiencing a number of consequences both physically and emotionally. When we get 7 to 8 hours of sleep, we are more creative, have more energy, experience better health and perform better than people who don't.

6. Eat Well

Healthy food options are more widely available than they have been in the last 50 years. Most grocery stores have entire sections devoted to healthy eating. Be intentional with what you eat. The saying is true: "You are what you eat". You can't expect to be in top shape both mentally and physically if all you eat is garbage.

7. Keep a Journal

It doesn't have to be lengthy and can include anything you would like to track, summarize or reflect on. I personally use Evernote (https://evernote.com/) and it has been a game changer for structuring my mind and prioritising my goals. If you are a leader, which you are, journaling is important as you grow and process through change and decisions. I find that journaling helps me think more clearly and balanced. Keep a record of your pursuit of excellence. Be flexible, but consistent.

8. Community

We all need a good inner circle and community. Family, the right friends and colleagues are crucial to a life of excellence. They help us to flourish. The people around me speak wisdom into my life, share ideas and serve as a sounding board. They support and encourage me. They show me love and tough love when needed to keep me on track. Feeling accepted and having at least one or two people that you can go to with anything will carry you through the good and turbulent times.

9. The Power Of Rest

Do you look forward to the weekends or vacations? Mentally and physically, we need rest. Our bodies know this and give us reminders when we have been pushing too hard. Listen to your body and know that resting is powerful.

10. Play

As we grow up, we can easily forget that this is essential to a life of excellence. Play inspires our creativity. It rejuvenates us. It enables mental agility and problem solving. These are all essential for pursuing excellence. Play games or sports. Explore and go on an adventure to somewhere new. Do something artistic. Most importantly, smile, laugh and have fun; life is intended to be enjoyed and not endured.

11. Learn Something New Everyday

If you want to live a life of excellence, you have to keep learning and growing. We live in a time where learning new skills is one-click away. Knowledge is power and crucial in your journey to excellence.

Worth The Work

You are probably already utilizing some of these habits. You may just do them once in a while but the key to habits is consistency. However, as Benjamin Franklin found out, we can really only create one or two new habits at a time. Pick a new habit to develop, one that you think will really make a difference for you. Work at it; solidify it. Where do you want your habits to lead you? Make time to clarify your destination and then analyse if you current habits are taking you there or you have to learn new habits.

Chapter 16
Not Above Average

"You don't have to like it, you just have to do it." ~ *Navy Seals*

Kobe Bryant, one of the best basketball players in history was famous for his work ethic. While everyone else was sleeping, he was hitting the gym or practicing shots pre-game and post-game. Excellence at its finest! Almost every world-class, high-performance organization takes training seriously. Similarly like Kobe Bryant, Navy Seals go uncomfortably beyond the norm in training and preparation. They are obsessive and obsessed. They are arguably the best in the world at what they do. Their dedication to relentless training and intensive preparation, however, is far from the norm within a majority of the businesses or professional minds.

Real-world excellence requires more than commitment to educational achievement or training. The Navy Seal's leadership recognized that technical excellence; better shooting and better shots didn't go nearly far enough in addressing the complex environments and demands that would be made upon sniper teams in wartime deployments. The wartime challenge demanded better collaboration, greater situational awareness and more strategic application of cutting edge technology for the war-fighter.

The Navy Seals apply 4 transformational training themes that should be applied in every organisation and personal life. In their training programme, they took best practices from teaching, professional sports, and even Olympic champions:

1. Produce Excellence, Not Above Average

Being very good is just not good enough. We should never try to achieve "good enough" or "above average". Instead we must always choose to be dedicated to producing excellence. Serious organizations don't aspire to be comfortably above average, they want to be the best.

"Training divorced from excellence is mere compliance." ~ Michael Schrage (Harvard Business Review)

Aiming for above average is more "box ticking" than human capital investment. Is above average training really worth the time, energy and expense? A kaizen, continuous improvement, ethos is one thing. But customer service and leadership training that only enhances rather than transforms capabilities and skills are just not good enough or sustainable. Do companies really want training to empower and bring out the best in their people? Or does everyone train with the tacit expectation that excellence matters less than being a bit better?

2. Incentivize Excellence Not Competence

If training itself is world-class, organizations need recognition and rewards systems that explicitly acknowledge and promote excellence. When I started my career at a large consulting firm, there was an "up-or-out" culture, which simply put meant that if you didn't get better each year, you could look for another job. Such culture means that leaders and organisations need to have the courage and integrity to reposition and replace those who can't or won't step up. Should personal development and training overwhelmingly focus on skills enhancement? Or must it be managed to build better bonds and relationships throughout the enterprise? Both are important, because they will result in a culture that is more open to innovation and exchange. Incentives aligning and facilitating accountability will improve the entire organization.

3. Incorporate New Ideas from the Ground

Learning is a continuous process that never stops and new ideas can come from the ground up, meaning from all levels. Successful training must be dynamic, open and innovative. Ongoing transformation, not just incremental improvement, is what brings an entire organisation to the next level. I learned, even as CEO, that you are never done learning, and your team can be a wealth of information to improve the business.

4. Lead by Example

Getting better at getting better is a vital principle for organizations to keep on learning. This is a culture and mindset that needs to be cultivated. The most important behaviour a leader can demonstrate, is to lead by example. Great leaders are not too proud to step out of their ivory tower and lead the team into the battlefield. If you do it right, your team will respect you and follow you. Lead by example and watch your team elevate you with their accomplishments. Leading by example is what truly empowers small teams and teamwork.

In Special Operations (Navy Seals) environments and top business environments, you have the privilege of working with people who just get the job done at all costs. They are self-motivators. Even if they don't have the know-how, they will figure it out and just make it happen. When we first launched our website, we pulled a couple of all-nighters with the whole team and it was amazing to see a team that just wants to make things happen. It was amazing to see what they accomplished together. The level of motivation, dedication and self-sacrifice the Navy Seals demand from themselves and each other goes far, far beyond what most businesses should ever ask, let alone expect, from their people. But that said, for leaders and managers who truly care about their people and their customers, the Navy Seals culture of excellence is a great example. Nobody doubts the vital role consistent training and education play in creating and sustaining a level of excellence and economic competitiveness worldwide.

Chapter 17
Building G.R.I.T.

"Greatness requires internal toughness." ~ *Anonymous*

Last set. I honestly feel like hitting the shower and just put on some Netflix and chill on the couch. My muscles already burn like they are on fire but I got one more set to go and then I am done for today. That last set always kills me. Heartbeat is up. Sweat is pouring and face is all red, but I give it all I got! Every time I go to the gym, I encounter that feeling of almost wanting to give up when I try to push myself a bit further. Building perseverance is a core skill for any leader and something every company should focus on embedding in the company culture.

How do you grow excellence, passion, ownership and perseverance at the same time? This question actually comes down to building GRIT within your personal and professional life. GRIT being a combination of passion, resilience, determination, and focus that allows a person to maintain the discipline and optimism to persevere in difficult times.

The more perseverance, ownership and passion; the stronger the organisation, the better the efficiency, the happier the people and the stronger the numbers. One of the key ingredients to greatness is GRIT.

"…High but not the highest intelligence, combined with the greatest degree of persistence, will achieve greater eminence than the highest degree of intelligence with somewhat less persistence." ~ Angela Duckworth (professor and author)

How do you build more GRIT to achieve excellence? 6 steps to building more GRIT:

1. **Pursue what interests you**. A lot of myths surround this topic and especially millennials like to float around, finding their passion and interests. They start to daydream and ponder hours, days, weeks and years about what they are passionate about. Wrong! Introspection is not the right path. You need to get out there and try stuff so you really know what is perfect for you. You don't just like the idea of doing it, but actually like doing it with all failures and struggles that come along.

Having the right mentor is key to turning passion into a skill because interest precedes the development of talent.

2. **Practice**. One of the key strengths of Navy Seals is the culture of constant self-improvement and focus on training. "90% of every post-mission debrief is focusing on what they did wrong or could have done better." ~ James Waters, Navy Seal. People need 10.000 hours to reach expertise level in any subject. To achieve that, you need to practice, practice and practice. Deliberate practice is intense and intentional.

3. **Purpose**. GRIT people find purpose in what they do, which makes them significantly more motivated than others. Interest without purpose is not sustainable. GRIT people don't just have a job, they have a calling. Three bricklayers were asked, "What are you doing?" The first said, "I'm laying bricks". The second said, "I'm building a church". The third said, 'I'm building the house of God". This is the difference between a job, career and calling.

4. **The best is yet to come**. To build GRIT, people need to believe and have active hope that the best is yet to come.

5. **High Hopes.** Research[37] shows that those lacking hope typically adopt performance goals and choose easy tasks that don't offer a challenge or opportunity for growth. When they fail, they quit. They act helpless and life always happens to them instead of for them. When people have hope for a better tomorrow, they build a better stamina to keep moving forward during the ups and downs.

6. **Choose a GRITTY inner circle**. We are social beings, and are influenced by our social environment. Social pressure can be awesome if you use it in the right way. So hang with the right people and it will rub off on you. Over time and under the right circumstances, the norms and values of the group to which we belong become our own. We internalise them. We carry them with us, so be intentional with your inner circle.

---

[37] https://www.cnbc.com/id/100537689

Exercise: Excellence

1. Identify 3 projects (business or personal) that you are working on. Example: Getting in physical shape.
2. Describe an excellent version of those projects. Example: Losing 5 KG and drop BMI to 23.
3. Big milestones: Break the project in big milestones. Example: Focus on improving strength in biceps and chest, eating healthy, meditation and getting lean with yoga.
4. Micro actions: Make a daily focus on reaching each big milestone. Example: Spend the first 15 minutes of the day with a short exercise, 50 x push-ups.

Macro goals:

1. _____

2. _____

3. _____

Big milestones:

1. _____

2. _____

3. _____

Micro actions:

1. _____

2. _____

3. _____

IGNITE: All Systems Go

"In the end, it is important to remember that we cannot become what we need to be by remaining who we are." ~ Max De Pree (businessman and author)

Throughout this book I have talked about the 6 steps to ignite millennial leadership. I discuss leadership in both your professional career and personal life because leadership starts within in you. How do you lead your life? How do you set a vision of where you want to go in life? How will you impact the people around you? How do you grow your influence? The goal of this book was to give you a tool on your leadership journey. Some people say, "not everyone can be a leader", and I partly agree with that because there are many nuances to this statement. I agree that maybe not everyone is suited to become the president of a country, run a billion dollar company or become the next Christiano Ronaldo. But there is so much in between.

At the end of the day, I believe that we are all called to lead. It is not so much about your capacity; it is more about how you leverage your ability. The people that don't focus too much on their capacity and limitations, will achieve great things. It all starts by leading your life and understanding yourself better by growing self-awareness and understanding your strengths and weaknesses.

We all have the ability to inspire, but we need to be aware of that power before we can use it. The moment we understand our own capacity to inspire, the better we can push the right buttons to influence and engage with people.

Your mindset determines how you see the world. Therefore having a growth mindset is crucial in your leadership journey. Just like the human body is able to regenerate itself, you can recondition your mind towards a growth mindset. The moment we catch our thinking to fall into fixed mindset responses, isolate it and fight back with growth mindset answers. Just by adding "yet" to your vocabulary is already powerful and turn fixed mindset thoughts into growth mindset thoughts. If you are not able to perform a certain task, just say, "I can't do it, *yet*!" instead of "I can't do it." Just by adding these three letters, you tell your brain that your current capacity is just based on today's circumstances and you believe there is room for improvement. Tomorrow is a better day, and the future is bright but we need to repeat this self-talk to our brain so that continuous growth and development become the new norm.

Kobe Bryant was at the top of his basketball career and winning trophy after trophy. This did not stop him from putting in the extra hours, nurturing the right mindset and training hard. Once we move into a leadership mindset, we need to keep nurturing the right mindset and expose our mind and body to the uncomfortable zone so we can keep growing. In today's transparent world, you are either influencing others or are influenced by others. The moment we realise that we all have the ability to influence others, we become more intentional on how we do it. Use your influence, big or small, to create positive change and lift others.

The currency for any leader is trust. It builds relationships and makes a big difference in any organisation. Without trust there is no deep impact so we need to understand how we can build trust. Look for affiliation or common ground to find that first connection. Affiliation is the number one method that the world's best negotiators use in conflict resolution to build that initial trust between two parties. The good news is that the "affiliation" method is available for all of us. The moment we understand how to build trust, our influence grows.

Excellence is your new normal. Set your bar high and aim for excellence in everything you do. Two of the most important lessons that can be learned from the legendary Navy Seals are that we should always go for excellence and not above average, and always focus on improvements. Once we embrace these mindsets we are set to achieve greatness and awaken the leader within.

It these times of massive distractions where social media is sometimes perceived as the truth, it is a good reminder that it doesn't matter what people say. What matters most is what you say about yourself. I believe in your potential and sincerely hope that this book will be of value in your journey. I would like to end this book with a quote from Napoleon Hill.

"If you can't do great things. Do small things in a great way." ~ Napoleon Hill (author)

Let's start with small steps. Steps that are confident and lead the way to higher levels. All systems go.

Let's ignite that spark,

Your friend,

Andrew Senduk

About the Author

Andrew Senduk is an author, speaker and business strategist. He has inspired venues across the globe, from small executive leadership meetings to business conferences with thousands of people. His experience of both the corporate and start-up environment gives him a unique view on entrepreneurship and leadership. He started his career in Fortune 500 companies but fell in love with entrepreneurship. He has built companies from the ground up, literally from his living room, and scaled businesses to multi million dollar companies employing hundreds of people. Above all he is a family man that loves his wife Melissa and sons Rocco and Zion. He is passionate about next generation leadership and believes that millennials are the key to innovation, growth and the future. If you would like to work with Andrew or just want to connect with him, please contact him via the below links or send him some love on social media @asenduk.

Visit: www.andrewsenduk.com

Email: hello@andrewsenduk.com

Ignite Millennial Leadership

www.ingramcontent.com/pod-product-compliance
Lightning Source LLC
Chambersburg PA
CBHW071457220526
45472CB00003B/832